POCKET FACTFILES

Mammals

Project Director: **Graham Bateman**
Managing Editor: **Shaun Barrington**
Picture Manager: **Claire Turner**
Production: **Clive Sparling**
Design & Editorial: **Kinsey & Harrison**
Designer: **Edward Kinsey**
Editors: **James Harrison,**
 Louisa Somerville
Cartography: **Tim Williams**

Produced by
Andromeda Oxford Limited,
Kimber House, 1 Kimber Road
Abingdon, Oxfordshire OX14 1BZ
www.andromeda.co.uk

© copyright Andromeda Oxford Ltd 2003

Library of Congress Cataloging-in-
Publication Data Available

10 9 8 7 6 5 4 3 2 1

Published in 2003 by Sterling Publishing
Co., Inc.
387 Park Avenue South,
New York, NY 10016
Distributed in Canada by Sterling
Publishing,
c/o Manda Group,
One Atlantic Avenue, Suite 105
Toronto, Ontario, Canada M6K 3E7

Printed in Hong Kong

Sterling ISBN 1–4027–0293–0

Photographic Credits

Ardea Ian Beames 184–185;

Bruce Coleman Collection Stephen J.
Krasemann 33;

Frank Lane Picture Agency F.W. Lane 223;

Natural History Photographic Agency
T. Kitchen & V. Hurst 201;

Nature Picture Library Dietmar Nill 213; John
Cancalosi 237;

Oxford Scientific Films Norbert Rosing 6, 91;
Steve Turner 9; Mike Hill 10–11, 123; Frank
Schneidermeyer 13; John Downer 15; Fabio
Colombini/Animals Animals 19; Keith Ringland
23; Daniel J. Cox 27, 39, 41, 47, 56–57, 85; Alan
& Sandy Carey 35, 53, 173; Berndt Fischer 37,
163; Robin Redfern 51; Mark Hamblin 54–55, 95,
181; Tim Jackson 67; Will Darnell/Animals
Animals 71; Gerard Soury 75; David Fleetham 87;
Richard Herrmann 89; Howard Hall 93; Doug
Allan 97; Konrad Wothe 105; Martyn Chillmaid
107; Partridge Prod. Ltd. 115; Richard Packwood
117, 127; Martyn Colbeck 119, 125; Jorge Sierra
137; Niall Benvie 147; Stan Osolinski 149, 157;
Tom Ulrich 171, 175, 241; G.I. Bernard 187;
Rodger Jackman 197; Michael Powles 199; Joe
McDonald/Animals Animals 203; Tony Tilford
207; Terry Andrewartha/Survival Anglia 209;
Michael Fogden 219; Carlos Sanchez Alonso 227;
Hans & Judy Beste/Animals Animals 231;
Daybreak Imagery 233; Bert & Babs Wells 235;
Kathie Atkinson 249; Oxford Scientific Films 214.

A. Smith 245.

All artwork copyright Andromeda Oxford Ltd.

POCKET FACTFILES

Mammals

Sterling Publishing Co., Inc.
New York

CONTENTS

LARGE HERBIVORES 124

SMALL MAMMALS 172

MARSUPIALS & MONOTREMES 228

GLOSSARY 250 INDEX 254

THE DIVERSITY OF MAMMALS

IT IS DIFFICULT to imagine a more diverse group of living things than mammals. Compare the Central American smoky bat (*Furipterus horrens*), a tiny predator with a body not much longer than a bumble bee to the gargantuan blue whale (*Balanoptera musculus*), the size of several buses. The bat is covered in soft fur, moves through the air on membranous wings and snaps up prey in jaws lined with tiny teeth. The whale has only a sparse scattering of hairs, swims with languid strokes of its powerful tail, and strains planktonic crustaceans from the water with curtains of fibrous baleen hanging from the roof if its mouth.

Now compare both these extraordinary animals with another – this one lives on land and walks on two legs. It is medium-sized and really rather weak. Yet the large brain inside its round skull enables it to hunt other animals or train them to do its will. *Homo sapiens* is capable of complex, abstract thought and can communicate complex ideas with others of its kind. It can take to the air, dive the deep oceans, and even venture into the vacuum of space.

At first glance it might be easier to see the things that separate bat, whale, and human. Yet we are all mammals, and along with some 4,800 other species, we all evolved from the same common ancestor.

WALRUS
The walrus has no fur
– just a sparse scat-
tering of bristly hairs.
For warmth it relies
instead on a thick
layer of insulating fat.

What makes a mammal?

This is a more complicated question than it seems. While most of us instinctively recognize a mammal when we see one, it is less easy to come up with a completely failsafe description that takes into account the group's great diversity and excludes other kinds of animals. For example, mammals breathe air, but then so do reptiles. Mammals have warm blood – so do birds. There are exceptions and variations to most of the general rules used to define what makes a mammal, so the best approach is to use a combination of the following criteria and a little common sense.

PUMA
Cats such as the puma are out and out carnivores. When hunting they combine stealth, agility, and sharp teeth and claws to deadly effect.

• **Mammals keep a constant warm body temperature**. Some, however are warmer than others – marsupials generally operate at a lower body temperature than placental mammals, and hibernating dormice may allow their body temperature to drop close to freezing to save energy. Bears, too, hibernate at lower body temperatures.

• **Mammals generate body heat from within** (scientists use the term endothermic). However many species sometimes also use external sources of heat, such as the sun, to warm themselves and thus save energy.

• **Mammals have a body covering of hair or fur**. This is almost always true, though in some species, such as whales, naked mole rats, and some humans, the hair is so sparse as to be unnoticeable.

• **Mammals give birth to active babies.** True except for three species, all members of the Order Monotremata, that lay eggs. These are small, with a rubbery shell, and hatch after a few days into normal mammalian babies.

• **Mammals produce milk for their young from mammary glands**. Only half of all mammals do this. The rest are males!

In fact there is only one completely reliable criterion for identifying a mammal – this concerns the structure of the skull and jaw. There is just one lower jawbone (the dentary), which articulates directly to the skull. The skulls of mammals are all constructed this way, whereas those of other vertebrates, such as the reptiles, which share an ancient common ancestor with mammals, are not.

MANDRILL
The colorful nose of the dominant male mandrill has evolved over time as a symbol to other mandrills of his strength and high status.

The history of mammals

The first mammals appeared between 225 and 150 million years ago. Our ancestors belonged to an Order of reptiles called the *Therapsida*. Therapsids were small and nimble, with a lighter skeleton than most other reptiles. However the dawn of the mammals was hardly the grand event one might expect. For the first 100 million years or more, early reptile-like mammals remained small and inconspicuous – like mice below the stage at a grand opera house. For over 150 million years the bright lights of center stage belonged to another branch of the reptile lineage – the dinosaurs. It was only when these awesome creatures bowed out at the end of the Cretaceous period that mammals began to flourish.

Classifying mammals

The classification of living things, known as taxonomy, is a science in itself. Mammals are grouped together in the Class Mammalia, within which there are 28 subgroups, or Orders, which contain broadly similar animals, for example; Chiroptera (bats), Cetacea (whales and dolphins) and Rodentia (rodents). Orders are in turn split into families, families into genera (singular genus) and genera into species. The species in this book have been loosely grouped according to their lifestyle – marine mammals, hunters and scavengers, herbivores and so on; but their scientific classification is also given, so that taxonomic relationships can be established.

GIRAFFES
Because mammals care for their young, they tend to build stronger social bonds than many other kinds of animal. Giraffes live in casual groups.

LION

Panhera leo
Family: FELIDAE
Order: CARNIVORA

Gir Forest Sanctuary

DISTRIBUTION: Originally distributed from Africa to India, lions are now confined to the African grasslands and open woodlands south of the southern Sahara, and the Asian subspecies is restricted to the Gir Sanctuary in northwest India. The lions' status is not seriously threatened, but numbers are declining as a result of habitat loss.

SIZE: Length 5–8.2ft (1.4–2.5m); tail 2.3–3.3ft (70–100cm); height 2.6-3.6ft (80–110cm); weight 265–772lb (120-350kg). Males are larger than females.

APPEARANCE: The coat is light tawny, paler on the belly and inner legs, and the backs of the ears are black. The mane of the male ranges from tawny to black. Young cubs are marked with a pattern of rosettes.

DIET: Hoofed mammals, such as antelopes, gazelles, zebras, giraffes, and wild hog, also the young of larger animals like elephants and rhinos. Lions also scavenge from kills made by other predators.

BREEDING: Breeding is cooperative within a pride. Litters of 2–4 cubs arrive at any time of year after a gestation of 100–119 days. They are weaned at 6–7 months, but not completely independent of their mother until about 30 months old. Sexual maturity comes at 3–4 years, and longevity is up to 20 years in the wild (and up to 30 in captivity).

FEMALE HUNTERS
Lionesses do most of the hunting and often work in teams. The fastest females chase prey and the others lie in wait to ambush it.

LIFESTYLE: About 20 percent of African lions are nomadic and non-territorial, but most live in resident territorial prides. Lions are by far the most social of the cats. Prides are based on a group of related females, including sisters, daughters, mothers and grand-mothers. The adult males of the pride also tend to be related (brothers or cousins). They rarely stay with the pride more than three or four years before they are displaced by younger, stronger males. On taking over a pride, new males usually attempt to kill any young cubs in order to bring the lionesses into breeding condition once more. A receptive female may mate 50 or more times in 24 hours, usually but not always with the same male. When the new cubs arrive, both males and females treat them with great tolerance.

The lion's roar is just one of a varied repertoire of vocalizations. A full-blown roar is used to define territorial boundaries and can be heard by humans up to 5 miles (8km) away.

TIGER

Panthera tigris
Family: FELIDAE
Order: CARNIVORA

DISTRIBUTION: India, Southern China, Manchuria, Sumatra, Java, and Bali in tropical forests, swamps, and grasslands, but never far from water. Tigers have suffered from centuries of persecution and the remaining populations are threatened by habitat loss and illegal hunting. The species is listed as endangered.

SIZE: The world's largest cat. Length 55–110in (1.4–2.8m); height 31–43in (0.8–1.1m); tail 23–43in (0.6–1.1m); weight 65–300kg (143–660lb). Males can be up to twice as big as females. There is considerable size variation among the geographic subspecies, with the largest individuals in Siberia and the smallest in Bali.

APPEARANCE: A huge, highly muscular cat with a large head, long tail, and a striking orange coat with dark stripes.

DIET: Mainly large hoofed mammals including deer, buffalo, antelope, and gaur. Some individuals regularly kill and eat humans.

BREEDING: Cubs are born at any time of year, usually in litters of 2 or 3. Gestation lasts 95–110 days and the suckling period is 3–6 months. Females mature faster than males and first breed at 3–4 years. Males may mate at 4–5 years. Tigers rarely live more than 10 years in the wild.

LIFESTYLE: Apart from mothers with young families, which stay together two and a half years or more, tigers live alone. Individuals of the same sex tend not to occupy they same range. The size of home range varies hugely depending on the quality of habitat–anything from 8 to 1600 square miles (20–4,000sq km). Females occupy smaller ranges; there may be 3 or 4 living within the range of a single male. Tigers are territorial, but fights over land hardly ever happen. As long as the resident tiger keeps patrolling its territory and marking it with scent, others will respect its ownership. This is not to say that tigers are nonaggressive. Females are very protective of their young because males often try to kill cubs fathered by another in order to bring females into breeding condition more quickly.

Tigers are excellent climbers and swimmers and, unlike most cats, apparently relish being in the water. Tigers have long hind limbs and can leap up to 30 feet (10m) in a single bound. They can be active at any time of night or day, but most are primarily nocturnal.

CHEMICAL ANALYSIS
This is not just a yawn. The male is performing "flehmen," curling back the lips and raising the head to detect the reproductive status of a female through her urine traces.

CHEETAH

Acinonyx jubatus
Family: FELIDAE
Order: CARNIVORA

DISTRIBUTION: Savanna grassland, scrub and semidesert throughout sub-Saharan Africa, excluding the Congo Basin. Small population in Iran. The whole species is listed as Vulnerable due to the scattered nature of the population.

SIZE: Length 44–60in (112–150cm); height 26–37in (67–94cm); tail 23.5–31.5in (60–80cm); weight 46–159lb (21–72kg).

APPEARANCE: Cheetahs have a lean body and long slender legs. The head is small and the tail very long. The spine is remarkably flexible, allowing the cat to take huge strides and the paws have blunt, nonretractile claws that improve traction. The fur is short and pale gold to tawny brown, with black spots and dark bands on the end of the tail.

DIET: Mostly gazelles and impala, but other hoofed animals are hunted as the opportunities arise.

BREEDING: Cheetahs are sexually mature at about 18 months but rarely begin breeding before about 2 years old. Litters of 1–8 (usually 3–5) blind, helpless cubs are born at any time of year after a 90–95 day gestation. The cubs are kept hidden in long grass and moved often until they are old enough to follow their mother at about 5 weeks. They are weaned at 3–6 months, sexually mature at 18 months but rarely breed before 2 years. Infant mortality is high, up to 90 percent, but fortunate individuals may live 14 or 15 years.

LIFESTYLE: The cheetah is the fastest animal on four legs. On even ground it can reach speeds of 65mph (105kmh). Cheetahs can only keep up this astounding speed for about a minute and 3 out of every 4 hunts fail because the intended victim has too great a head start.

Female cheetahs live alone in large home ranges, which overlap with those of other females, and males. Males usually live in groups of 2 or 3, usually brothers. They are highly territorial and work together to defend an area within which they claim breeding rights. On finding a female in estrus, the males do not fight, but accept the right of one of them to mate.

SINGLE MOTHER
After mating, male cheetahs move on, leaving the females to rear the resulting cubs alone. Young cubs have long gray fur on their head, nape, and neck, but this disappears as they grow.

SNOW LEOPARD

> *Uncia uncia*
> Family: FELIDAE
> Order: CARNIVORA

DISTRIBUTION: Rocky mountain-sides and grassy alpine plateaus at 9,000–20,000 feet (2,700–6,000m) in the Himalayas, Altai and Hindu Kush. Declining as a result of hunting for fur and other body parts and persecution by farmers.

SIZE: Length 39–51in (1.0–1.3m); height 24in (60cm); tail 31–39in (80–100cm); weight 55–165lb (25–75kg); males half as big again as females.

APPEARANCE: A heavily built cat with relatively short legs, large feet, small head and a very long tail. The fur is very thick and pale gray to creamy white, with gray spots and rosettes providing excellent camouflage on rocky, snow-covered slopes.

DIET: Mountain mammals including ibex, wild sheep, goats, deer, pikas, and marmots; some domestic animals and large birds such as pheasants and ptarmigan. Also musk ox, wild boar, hares, and rodents. The size of their range depends of the local abundance of prey and can be anything from 5 to 400 square miles (12–1,000sq km).

BREEDING: Litters of 1–5 (usually 2 or 3) cubs are born between April and June after a 90–103 day gestation. They are reared in a rocky shelter lined with fur and weaned at 2–3 months. They are sexually mature at 2 years and live up to 21 years.

LATE RISER
Snow leopards are active from late afternoon through the night to early morning, and except for females with young, they live alone.

LIFESTYLE: The snow leopard's magnificent coat is one of many adaptations to life in high mountains. The fur is three inches thick and even covers the soles of the feet. The large feet spread the cat's weight so it can walk over soft snow. Snow leopards have large nostrils in which air is warmed as it is inhaled and cooled on the way out to reduce condensation that could turn to ice on the face. The fur on the face and head is not as thick as elsewhere so when the snow leopard is sleeping, it covers its nose with its long, furry tail. The tail also acts as a counterbalance and contributes to the animal's extraordinary agility. Snow leopards can leap around 20 feet (6m) into the air and cover up to 50 feet (15m) in a single forward bound. Unlike other "big cats," such as lions and leopards, snow leopards cannot roar.

JAGUAR

Panthera onca
Family: FELIDAE
Order: CARNIVORA

DISTRIBUTION: Near water in forest, grassland and semi desert regions of Central and South America, south to northern Argentina and Paraguay. Jaguars are no longer widely hunted for their skin but are still declining in range and population.

SIZE: The largest cat in the Americas; length 44–73in (1.12–1.85m); height 27–30in (680–760mm); tail 18–30in (450–750mm); weight 130–264lb (60–120kg). Males are larger than females.

APPEARANCE: A large, robustly built cat with a short, thick tail and a massive head. The coat is pale gold to reddish-brown with spots arranged in pattern of rosettes and rings. All-black or "melanistic" individuals are quite common.

DIET: Mostly medium-sized mammals such as peccaries, capybaras, tapirs and other mammals, crocodiles, and fish.

BREEDING: Litters of 1–4 cubs. Gestation lasts 93–105 days and the cubs are cared for by the mother alone. Young are weaned at 5–6 months and sexually mature at 2–4 years. Adults are solitary and territorial, but peaceful, and can live up to 24 years.

LIFESTYLE: Jaguars are most active around dawn and dusk but can be up and about at any time of day. They are superb climbers and often hunt and relax in the branches of trees. They are fond of waterside habitats and are excellent swimmers, but hunting is mostly done on dry land. Prey is killed with a crushing bite to the skull rather than breaking the neck or strangulation.

LEOPARD-LIKE
The jaguar has a broad, heavy-looking head. It is not unlike a leopard to look at – but with a stockier build and shorter tail.

BOBCAT

Felis rufus
Family: FELIDAE
Order: CARNIVORA

DISTRIBUTION: Throughout much of North America from southern Canada to central Mexico, in a wide variety of habitats including forest, swamps in low-lying and mountainous regions, and even in desert areas where some water is available. The species has declined as a result of persecution by humans.

SIZE: Length 25.5–41in (0.65–1.05m); height 17.5–23in (45–58cm); tail 4–7.5in (11–19cm); weight 9–33lb (4–15kg). Canadian bobcats are larger than those in the south of the species' range.

APPEARANCE: A small but robust cat with a short, "bobbed" tail and slender legs. The bobcat's thick fur and the ruff around its jowls make it look somewhat stocky. The fur is brownish gray with variable spots and streaks, including a black mark on the topside tip of the tail. There are short tufts of hair on the ears. The paws are large. The bobcat has a particularly fierce growl.

DIET: Small mammals and birds, sometimes larger prey such as small deer, some domestic animals.

BREEDING: 1–6 kittens are born in winter after a gestation of 60–70 days.

LIFESTYLE: Bobcats are typical cats – solitary, athletic, and resourceful. They are also true generalists and cope well in a wide variety of habitats and feed on almost any available prey. Bobcats can be active at any time of day, and they travel widely within their home range in search of food. They rely heavily on the element of surprise when hunting and are greatly helped by their mottled coat, which provides excellent camouflage. They pause frequently in their daily movements to leave scent marks, especially where their range borders that of another individual. Home ranges vary from 0.4–16 square miles (1–40sq km) but the largest ranges always belong to males. Perhaps because they have smaller ranges and fewer resources at their disposal, female bobcats are more territorial and their ranges do not overlap one another. The bobcat's range overlaps only slightly with that of the similar-looking lynx, which occupies colder habitats to the north.

Despite its relatively small size, the bobcat is quite fierce and equipped to kill animals as large as a deer. It roams freely at night and is frequently out and about during the day except at the peak of summer. It does not dig its own den. If a crevice or a cave is not available, it will inhabit a dense thicket or sometimes choose a hollow in a log or in a tree.

BOBCAT OR LYNX?
A good way to tell a bobcat from a lynx is the ear tufts, which are longer in the lynx, and the tip is entirely black on a lynx, while on the bobcat only the top side is marked.

WILD CAT

Felis silvestris
Family: FELIDAE
Order: CARNIVORA

European wild
cat distribution

DISTRIBUTION: Forests, scrub, open country, swamps, and coasts from Western Europe to southern Africa and central China including Scotland, several Mediterranean islands, the Middle East and India but excluding areas of desert and tropical rainforest. Despite this huge range, some subspecies are threatened.

SIZE: Length 20–30in (50–75cm); height 15–22in (38–56cm); tail 8–14in (21–35cm); weight 6.6–17.6lb (3–8kg).

APPEARANCE: A smallish cat, rather like a domestic tabby. The wild cat's tail is denser and thicker than a domestic cat's, and has a blunt tip.

DIET: Common prey items include mice, voles, and rabbits as well as birds, reptiles, and amphibians. Wild cats also eat small quantities of grass to help prevent the formation of hairballs in the stomach.

BREEDING: Female wild cats begin breeding at about 10 months. Breeding is confined to spring and early summer in temperate parts of the range but can happen all year round in the tropics. Gestation is 61–68 days, and the young are suckled for about 30 days. They can live to 13 years, but usually less.

LIFESTYLE: Wild cats are secretive, solitary and nocturnal. They prefer places where people are scarce. By day they sleep in dens, or occasionally emerge to bask in a secure sunny spot such as the branch of a tree. At night they roam around a home range of between 0.4 and 2 square miles (1–6sq km), using regular pathways and leaving scent marks as messages to other wild cats. The range will include several dens in rock crevices, tree hollows, or dense vegetation, and the cat will use whichever is convenient on any particular day.

They rarely venture outside their own home range, but will do so if food becomes scarce. Males are also tempted to wander in search of estrus females. They compete for the right to mate, but rarely before they are 2 or 3 years old.

SMALL BUT FIERCE
Despite their small size, wild cats are extremely ferocious. When angry or frightened they hiss, spit, and snarl, and lash out with sharp hooked claws.

PUMA

Felis concolor
Family: FELIDAE
Order: CARNIVORA

DISTRIBUTION: Widespread throughout North and South America in habitats as varied as forest and grassland, mountains, and swamps.

SIZE: Length 38–88in (0.95–1.95m); height 23.5–27.5in (60–70cm); tail 21–32in (53–82cm); weight 80–264lb (36–120kg). Males can be two or three times bigger than females.

APPEARANCE: A large, muscular cat with long legs and a long, sweeping tail. The head is relatively small with large, rounded ears. The coat color varies from silvery gray to dark tawny.

DIET: Mostly large mammals, especially deer, but also smaller prey such as rodents and hares. Lone adults that kill a large animal such as a deer can live off the carcass for 2 weeks.

BREEDING: Litters of 1–6 (usually 3 or 4) kittens are born between January and June after 90–96 day gestation. The mother cares for them alone in a secure den and suckles them for about 3 months. Juveniles disperse at about 18 months and are sexually mature at 2.5–3 years. Pumas live up to 21 years in captivity, but rarely more than 14 in the wild.

LIFESTYLE: Pumas are generally solitary. They wander widely within a fixed home range that can be anything up to 400 square miles (1,000sq km) in area, though those of females are usually much smaller. Individuals living in the same area often use overlapping home ranges but manage to avoid meeting up by leaving scent marks wherever they go.

The scent, which is produced by glands under the tail and deposited when the cat urinates, provides other pumas with information about the individual that produced it. Male pumas can tell from a female's scent when she is ready to mate. This is the only time they will actively seek each other's company, although young cats from the same litter may remain together for a few months after their mother has left them.

Despite their large size, pumas are extremely agile. They are accomplished climbers and often rest in trees or use them to ambush prey on the ground, dropping onto the victim's back and killing it with a powerful bite to the neck.

SURVIVOR
Hunted to extinction by livestock farmers in the eastern USA and Canada, the puma is not threatened in its remaining habitat.

GRAY WOLF

Canis lupus
Family: CANIDAE
Order: CARNIVORA

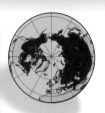

DISTRIBUTION: Throughout much of the northern hemisphere, excluding desert and tropical forest habitats. Formerly very widespread throughout the Northern hemisphere but now restricted to more remote areas of tundra, scrub, grassland, highland and forest. The population has stabilised following centuries of persecution.

SIZE: The largest species of dog; length 39–63in (1.0–1.60m); height 26–32in (66–81cm); tail 14–22in (35–56cm); weight 22–176lb (10–80kg). Males are larger than females and northern animals larger than those in the south of the species range.

APPEARANCE: A large, long-legged dog with thick, shaggy fur and a bushy tail. The fur is usually grey, though color varies from grayish to tawny-buff with paler underparts; some individuals may be reddish-brown to buff or black. This wolf is usually paler in northern regions.

DIET: Mainly large mammal prey including caribou and other deer, bison, moose, musk ox, mountain sheep, beavers, and hares. Wolves also eat carrion and seasonal fruits. A large wolf eats an average of 5.5lb (2.5kg) of meat a day.

BREEDING: 4–7 pups are born in den in late winter after a 63 day gestation period. They are weaned at 5 weeks and cared for by whole pack. Young wolves reach sexual maturity at 2 years, and may live as long as 16 years in the wild.

LIFESTYLE: This intelligent and adaptable predator usually lives in packs, often of around 20 animals, though loners and pairs are not uncommon in low latitude habitats. A wolf pack comprises a dominant breeding pair and their offspring of 1–2 years. The pack occupies a range from 8 square miles (20sq km) to a staggering 5,000 square miles (13,000sq km).

All pack members help defend the territory. Usually only the dominant pair breeds, while the non-breeders help care for the young. They bring food, watch over the pups while they play and protect them from harm. Dominance in the pack is established by threatening behavior and fighting. Gray wolves are largely nocturnal animals.

CALL OF THE WILD
Wolves keep in touch with the pack, or warn other wolves to keep out of their territory, by howling. Howling in unison makes the pack seem larger than it really is. Lone wolves rarely howl. The coyote or prairie wolf is a smaller relative of the gray wolf.

COYOTE

Canis latrans
Family: CANIDAE
Order: CARNIVORA

DISTRIBUTION: Common and widespread on North American grasslands and prairie, scrub and forest. Lowland populations may migrate into mountains in summer.

SIZE: Length 30–39in (75–100cm); tail 12–19in (30–40cm); Weight: 15–44lb (7–20kg). Size varies with habitat quality; males are usually larger than females.

APPEARANCE: Wolflike animal with large pointed ears, narrow muzzle, slender legs and small feet. Running coyotes carry their tail in a low sweep, not straight out like a wolf. Shaggy fur is beige or gray, paler on belly, but usually darkens to black on tip of tail. Males are slightly larger than females.

DIET: About 90 percent meat, with some fruits taken in season. Prey varies with habitat, but includes rabbits, woodchucks, rodents and deer. Hunting for small animals is a solitary activity but where large prey is plentiful coyotes hunt in cooperative packs. They sometimes kill livestock.

BREEDING: Coyotes reach sexual maturity at 1 or 2 years of age but tend not to breed before they have secured a personal territory.

UNPOPULAR WITH HUMANS
The adaptable and intelligent coyote is unpopular with farmers because of a perceived threat to livestock. The species also carries rabies and other animal diseases.

Pairs form a bond that may last from one season to life. Litters of 2–12 (average 6) pups are born in spring after a 2-month gestation period and are weaned at 5–6 weeks. Young are fed and protected by both parents. The young may remain with their parents to help rear the next litter of cubs. Maximum longevity in the wild is about 15 years.

LIFESTYLE: Coyotes are close cousins of gray and red wolves and are able to interbreed with both. Usually they are separated by different habitat preferences, but the coyote's great adaptability means its range has expanded at the expense of its larger relatives. Coyotes communicate using barks, whines, and howls, and by scent. They have excellent hearing and eyesight and a keen sense of smell. Their lifestyles vary enormously throughout the species' range. In northern Mexico adults live alone or in pairs, hunt rabbits and rodents and usually weigh less than 25lb (12kg). By the Canadian tundra coyotes live in family packs, hunt caribou and wapiti and almost grow twice as big as those in the south.

SILVER-BACKED JACKAL

Canis mesomelas
Family: CANIDAE
Order: CARNIVORA

DISTRIBUTION: Africa, in dry grassland and open woodland from Sudan to South Africa.

SIZE: Length 16.5–35.5in (45–90cm); height 12–19in (30–48cm); tail 10–16in (26–40cm); weight 13–29lb (6–13.5kg). Males are about 10 percent bigger than females.

APPEARANCE: A slender, fox-like wolf with long legs, a pointed face and large, triangular ears. The coat is rough and russet brown with a white-rimmed black saddle streaked with silvery gray, which extends to tip of tail.

DIET: A very varied diet including mammals such as rodents and small antelope. Also carrion, invertebrates, fruits, and other plant material.

MOTHER'S HELPER
Juveniles play-fighting; young silver-backed jackals often remain with their parents for a year or two, and help rear the next litter. They bring food to support the cubs, protect them from predators, play with them and stop them wandering too far.

BREEDING: 1–8 (usually 4) young are born after a 60-day gestation. Weaning takes place at 8–9 weeks, and young animals are sexually mature at 11 months. Jackals occasionally live 12 years or more but usually less than 8 in the wild.

LIFESTYLE: Silver-backed jackals are active at any time of day. Young animals use large home ranges but having found a mate they usually settle down and demarcate a smaller joint territory using howling and scent marks. After scent-marking their territory, the pair will patrol it together to prevent others trespassing. The pair bond may last a lifetime.

As well as living in pairs, silver-backed jackals also congregate in small family groups; and even greater numbers may gather around large carcasses. Within a territory there will be several dens, and litters of young are moved every few days as a precaution against predation. Jackals remain in close-knit family groups and all share in the duties of looking after the cubs and providing food for them.

Jackals have a reputation for killing spring lambs, and as a result, they are often persecuted in sheep-rearing areas by farmers trying to prevent attacks on livestock.

RED FOX

Vulpes vulpes
Family: CANIDAE
Order: CARNIVORA

DISTRIBUTION: Foxes are widespread throughout Europe and North America, and in parts of Africa and Asia in habitats as varied as farmland, forest, tundra, and urban areas. Ideal fox territory includes a mosaic of habitats. They have been introduced to Australia and New Zealand where they pose a serious threat to native wildlife.

SIZE: Length 18–35.5in (45–90cm); tail 12–21.5in (30–55cm); weight 6.5–31lb (3–14kg).

APPEARANCE: A delicately proportioned dog with a narrow body and a pointed face with erect triangular ears. The tail is thick and bushy. The coat is a variable shade of red from dark gold to dark brown, fading to white on muzzle, chest, belly, and tail tip; and often darker on legs.

DIET: Foxes are opportunist predators and will hunt almost anything. In practice they eat mostly rodents and other small mammals, insects, and worms. They also eat fruit in season and scavenge from human trash.

BREEDING: Cubs are born in litters of 1–13 (usually 3–7) after 52–53 days gestation. They are weaned at 8–10 weeks old, and sexually mature at 10 months. Generally they do not breed until they have dispersed and established a home range. They can live up to 12 years in captivity but rarely survive more than 5 in the wild.

LIFESTYLE: Fox foraging techniques range from collecting ripe fruit in late summer to plucking worms from the earth on damp evenings. However, the species is best known as an active and effective predator, using a combination of stealth, speed, and agility to catch small to medium sized mammals and birds. Foxes very rarely kill more than they need. Excess food is stored in a safe place, usually in a hole in the ground, so that it can be eaten later. Territories are marked with smelly urine and droppings.

FRIEND OR FOE?
The red fox is among the world's most adaptable carnivores. Its ability to live almost anywhere people can has given it a reputation for cunning and may bring it into conflict with humans.

ARCTIC FOX

Alopex lagopus
Family: CANIDAE
Order: CARNIVORA

DISTRIBUTION: Arctic regions of Canada, Alaska, Greenland, Iceland, Finland, Sweden, Norway, and Russia, on tundra and in boreal forests. They also venture onto ice caps and onto sea ice in winter.

SIZE: Length 18–27in (46–68cm); height 11in (28cm); weight 3–20lb (1.4–9kg).

APPEARANCE: A stout-looking little fox with short legs, small, rounded ears, and a thick, woolly coat. The tail is long and exceptionally bushy and the feet are furry. There are 2 color varieties: white foxes are only white in the winter, in summer they are grayish-brown; blue foxes have steely gray fur, darker in summer than in winter.

DIET: Prey includes seals, rodents (especially lemmings), sea birds, fish, invertebrates, and carrion. The species also scavenges from kills made by other arctic predators (i.e. wolves and polar bears). They occasionally eat plant material and other organic matter including the feces of other animals.

BREEDING: Females give birth to litters of 6–12 (occasionally as many as 25) pups in early summer after a 49–57 days gestation. They rely on help from their mate to rear such large families. The pups are weaned at 2–4 weeks and sexually mature at 10 months. They can live up to 16 years in captivity, but longevity is much less in the wild.

LIFESTYLE: During the winter many Arctic foxes undertake long journeys out onto the frozen sea, following polar bears. They are often entirely dependent on leftover bear kills, from which they scavenge whatever they can.

Farther south, lemmings form the staple diet, and Arctic fox population dynamics closely follow the cyclic boom and bust of lemming populations. In times of plentiful food the foxes put on a lot of weight. A thick layer of fat under the skin helps keep them warm and allows them to survive long periods without eating. Arctic foxes do not hibernate but if starving, they become much less active and are able to reduce their metabolic rate by about 50 percent to save energy.

Arctic foxes use snow holes to rest in winter but they maintain extensive dens on land for breeding. These are often used by generations of foxes, some for hundreds of years.

EXTREMELY WARM COAT
Arctic foxes are supremely adapted for cold weather. Their very thick fur, 70 percent of which is a fine, warm undercoat, is the warmest of any mammal. Individuals are able to tolerate temperatures as low as -70°F (-50°C) and lower. These young adults (showing the white winter coat color form) are play-fighting.

AFRICAN WILD DOG

> *Lycaon pictus*
> Family: CANIDAE
> Order: CARNIVORA

DISTRIBUTION: Savanna grassland and open woodland in sub-Saharan Africa. The species is declining in range and population and is listed as Endangered.

SIZE: Length 30–44in (0.75–1.12m); height 24–30in (61–78cm); tail 12–16 in (30–41cm); weight 37.5–80lb (17–36kg).

APPEARANCE: A lean, long-legged dog with large ears and four toes on each foot. The fur is short and thin and patterned with an almost endless variety in different blotches and speckles of black, brown, yellow, and white.

DIET: Mostly hoofed mammals including duikers, impalas, gazelles, gnus, and zebra.

BREEDING: Usually only the dominant pair of a pack is allowed to breed. Litters of up to 20 pups (usually 4–8) are born at any time of year after 79–80 days gestation. They are weaned by 11 weeks, and sexually mature within 2 years. The pups are doted on by all members of the pack, who provide food and take turns babysitting while the rest go hunting. Wild dogs live up to 17 years.

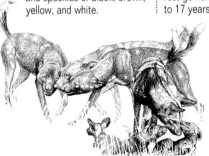

PATTERNED COAT
The African wild dog has a highly variable coat. The pattern helps break up the animal's outline but is probably just as important in individual recognition as in camouflage.

LIFESTYLE: African wild dogs are highly social. Most male dogs spend their whole lives in the same pack. There are more males than females in a pack and they are usually all related. Females on the other hand, disperse as young adults and compete for breeding rights, sometimes fighting to establish dominance in a new pack.

Once the social hierarchy is established however, the wild dog pack is a model of cooperative living. Members share responsibility for the young and even sick and injured adults that cannot hunt are taken care of. The dogs hunt as a team and always share their food amicably. Pups are given priority at kills. Prior to every hunt the pack engages in a lively greeting ritual, as if reaffirming their commitment to one another.

For most of the year the dogs are nomadic. They travel widely and their annual range can be as large as 1,500 square miles (4,000sq km). The range will overlap with those of neighboring packs, and the dogs do not bother to mark out territory. During the breeding season they wander less, and even nonbreeding animals stay close to the breeding den.

DINGO

Canis lupus dingo
Family: CANIDAE
Order: CARNIVORA

DISTRIBUTION: Australia, New Guinea, Indonesia, Borneo, Malaysia, Myanmar (Burma), Thailand, and the Philippines. Dingoes live in deserts, tropical and temperate forest, mountains, and farmland. The non-native status of Australian dingoes means that they are not entitled to protection and are killed when their hunting threatens livestock; their genetic integrity is compromised by interbreeding with domestic dogs.

SIZE: Length 2.8–4ft (0.86–1.22m); height 17–25in (44–63cm); tail 10–15in (26–38cm); weight 22–53lb (10–24kg).

APPEARANCE: A large dog with pricked ears and a slightly bushy tail. The fur is reddish gold with pale markings on feet, chest, muzzle, and tail tip.

DIET: Dingoes are not at all fussy and will eat whatever is available – including kangaroos, rabbits, lambs, insects, carrion, and fruit.

BREEDING: Often only the dominant female will be allowed to breed, and other pack members help care for the young. Litters of 1–10 (average 5) pups are born in an underground den during winter after a 63 day gestation period. The young are fully weaned at 3 months and sexually mature at 2 years of age. In good habitat longevity can be as much as 14 years.

LIFESTYLE: Dingoes are hardy and adaptable animals that use wily canine intelligence to eke out a living in the poorest of habitats. Like wolves, they are sociable and usually live in territorial packs. They hunt alone for small prey and as a pack for larger animals such as kangaroos. When natural prey is in short supply, dingoes often resort to hunting livestock. Territory size depends on habitat quality, with desert packs needing three times as much space to meet their needs as those living in wetter forested areas. The territory is maintained by scent marking and howling. Females usually remain with the pack in which they were born for life, while males disperse in search of a mate.

ABORIGINAL ARRIVAL
Dingoes were introduced to Australia by early Aboriginal settlers about 4,000 years ago. Similar animals still live throughout Southeast Asia and even in the US.

BROWN BEAR

Ursus arctos
Family: USIDAE
Order: CARNIVORA

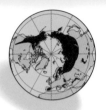

DISTRIBUTION: The most widespread bear on Earth, spanning three continents, brown bears inhabit tundra and open grassland in northwest North America, northern Europe and the mountains of southern Europe, the Middle East, and central Asia. The species is threatened by hunting.

SIZE: Length 67–111in (1.7–2.8m); tail 2.5–8in (6–21cm); height 35–60 in (0.9–1.5m); weight 132–1700lb (60–780kg). Size varies with geographic location, though males are bigger than females.

APPEARANCE: Large bear with thick, blond to black shaggy fur, often with gray- or silver-tipped hairs (grizzled) – hence the grizzly bear name in North America.

DIET: a true omnivore eating all kinds of food: grasses, herbs, fruits, berries, nuts and seeds; insects and honey; rodents; fish; also carrion; occasionally young hoofed mammals and livestock.

BREEDING: Litters of 1–4 (usually 2) cubs are born in late winter after a gestation of 210–255 days. They are weaned at 5 months and begin breeding at 4–6 years old. Longevity is up to 50 years. 1–4 cubs born in late winter .

LIFESTYLE: Brown bears are solitary and non-territorial, but will fight for dominance where access to a feeding resource is at stake. Aggression towards humans is rare and usually involves a mother with cubs to protect. Despite their huge bulk, brown bears are very agile and can run with surprising speed. The prominent nose and small eyes indicate that they rely more on smell to seek food rather than eyesight. They use their huge claws to dig for food and excavate hibernation dens. They swim well, and on the northwestern seaboard they "fish" salmon swimming upstream to spawn. However, they are not adept climbers.

THE HIBERNATOR Hibernation lasts from three to seven months of the year depending on the severity of the winter. In southern parts of the species range bears remain active all winter long.

POLAR BEAR

Ursus maritimus
Family: URSIDAE
Order: CARNIVORA

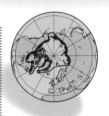

DISTRIBUTION: Polar bears roam within the Arctic Circle, including parts of Canada, Alaska, Russia, Scandinavia, and Greenland. They occupy sea ice, ice caps, and tundra, and are just as comfortable in water as on land.

SIZE: Length 80–100in (2.0–2.5m); height up to 63in (1.6m); tail 3–5in (7–13cm); weight 330–1760lb (150–800kg). Males are truly massive – usually much larger than females and the largest of all terrestrial predators. Large size is an adaptation to the cold and allows polar bears to tackle large prey, such as seals.

APPEARANCE: A huge bear with a thick, off-white coat. The head is relatively small, but the feet are large and covered with fur, even the soles.

DIET: Mainly ringed seals, occasionally other animals, such as

harp and bearded seals, young walrus and beluga whales, reindeer, fish, and seabirds. In summer they also eat leaves and berries.

BREEDING: Females give birth to litters of between 1 and 3 (occasionally 4) in the middle of winter after a 195–265 day gestation. The cubs begin to be weaned from 6 months, and become sexually mature at 5–6 years. Polar bears can live up to 45 years in captivity, 30 in the wild.

LIFESTYLE: Polar bears hunt seals by ambushing them at breathing holes or sneaking up on them as they rest on the ice. They also sniff out seal pups lying in dens under the ice and smash the roof with their front feet to get in. The bears wander widely, but they are not true nomads as was once believed. Individual bears do use regular home ranges, but these are vast – up to 200,000 square miles (500,000sq km). They spend their summers on land and move out onto the ice when the sea freezes over in winter. Most polar bears remain active throughout the winter, but pregnant females sleep all winter in large dens and give birth while they sleep. The newborn find their own way to their mother's teats and she suckles them for 4 months without ever waking up. In spring when the family emerges the mother is close to starvation.

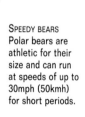

SPEEDY BEARS
Polar bears are athletic for their size and can run at speeds of up to 30mph (50kmh) for short periods.

RING-TAILED COATI

Nasua nasua
Family: PROCYONIDAE
Order: CARNIVORA

DISTRIBUTION: Wooded areas from Colombia east of the Andes in South America to northern Argentina and Uruguay.

SIZE: Length 16–26in (41–67cm); height up to 12in (30cm); tail 12–28in (32–69cm); weight 6.5–13lb (3–6kg). Males are usually rather larger than females.

APPEARANCE: The body is stocky with long back legs, a long, slender, banded tail and a long, flexible snout. The tail can be longer than the body. The coat is tawny brown, darker on the face with pale markings on cheeks, chin and throat. The ring-tailed coati has a small white spot above and below each eye, and a large one on each cheek.

DIET: Fruit and woodland invertebrates such as ants, termites, beetles, centipedes, grubs, spiders, and scorpions; also frogs, lizards, small mammals, and birds' eggs.

BREEDING: Litters of 2–7 in a tree nest between April and June after a 74 day gestation. Young are weaned at 4 months and sexually mature at 2 years. Coatis may live up to 15 years.

LIFESTYLE: Coatis are intelligent, social and highly inquisitive animals. The Latin name *Nasua* means "nosy one" and coatis use their long, sensitive snout to rummage about in the leaf litter for food. Coatis are mainly active during the day. They are nimble climbers, and can descend tree trunks headfirst like squirrels.

Female and juvenile coatis live in groups of up to 20 animals. Females help care for one another's young, and band members engage in mutual grooming, using teeth and claws to remove parasites. Communication is by chittering noises, and barking calls serve to warn of predators. Mature male coatis live alone except during the

FEMALE COMMUNES
These forest-dwelling relatives of the raccoons tend to live in all-female groups and share the maternal duties.

breeding season, when they are tolerated by females for breeding purposes. They are also permitted to inspect newborns and become familiarized with their own offspring. This appears to be a precaution against infanticide and cannibalism.

Male coatis look much the same as females, but their solitary life-style is so different to the sociable existence of females and young they were once thought to be a different kind of animal altogether. They were known as "coatimundis", and the name is still used by many people.

COMMON RACCOON

Procyon lotor
Family: PROCYONIDAE
Order: CARNIVORA

DISTRIBUTION: Found throughout North and Central America in forest, scrub, and urban areas.

SIZE: Length 18–28in (45–68cm); height 10–12in (25–30cm); tail 8–12in (20–30cm); weight 11–33lb (5–15kg). Females are about 25 percent smaller than males and southern animals are smaller than northern ones.

APPEARANCE: The face has black eyes, short, rounded ears which are light-tipped, and a black "bandit mask" – a face mask with gray or whitish bars above and below. The tail is bushy with alternate brown and black rings, while the rest of the body is grizzled gray or reddish-gray. The forepaws look like little hands.

DIET: Raccoons eat just about anything including fruits, berries, nuts, seeds, fish, crayfish, clams, snails, and earthworms, crops such as maize and stored grain and any kitchen scraps left as garbage.

Raccoons are often called bandits, not just for their face mask but also for their habit of raiding garbage cans, food stores, and farmers' crops – leaving a trail of rubbish behind them.

BREEDING: Births peak from February to April, when litters of 4–6 young are born in a nest or den. Gestation lasts 63 days and weaning begins at 7 weeks. Females are usually ready to breed within their first spring. Raccoons may live up to 16 years.

LIFESTYLE: Raccoons are adaptable opportunists. They are able to make a meal from almost anything and are most active at night. In towns they are notorious for raiding garbage bins for food scraps. Their normal gait is a slow, waddling walk, but they can run fast when necessary. They are strong swimmers and excellent climbers. They use dens in hollow trees, burrows, log piles and buildings to shelter and rear young. Raccoons do not hibernate, but in northern regions they may spend much of the winter in their dens, which are usually in hollow trees or abandoned burrows. A female and her offspring often hunt independently but den together. At other times adult raccoons are generally solitary. In the breeding season rival males may fight and fighting raccoons make a variety of fierce growls, snarls, and squeaks.

HANDS-ON SKILLS
Raccoons are very nimble fingered. Their forepaws are more like hands and are used for catching food and for grooming. They are dexterous enough to manipulate very small objects and they can even untie knots.

COMMON WEASEL

Mustela nivalis
Family: MUSTELIDAE
Order: CARNIVORA

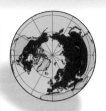

DISTRIBUTION: Throughout the northern hemisphere including Canada, Alaska, Siberia, Japan, northern United States, Greenland, Iceland, Scandinavia, northern Europe and Russia, occupying habitats as varied as meadows, farmlands, thickets, prairies, marshes, and open woodland.

SIZE: The smallest member of the Order Carnivora; length 4.3–10in (11–25cm); tail 0.7–3in (17–80mm); weight 0.9–8oz (25–240g). Males are larger than females and Eurasian animals generally grow bigger than North American ones.

APPEARANCE: A long, sleek-bodied animal with short legs and a short tail. The head is flattened with large black eyes and neat round ears. The coat is reddish-brown and separated from creamy-white underparts with a clear demarcation line. In northern populations the fur turns completely white in winter. The common weasel may have dark blotches on its underparts. The tail is reddish-brown.

DIET: Mainly small rodents such as mice, voles, and lemmings. Also moles, pikas, birds, fish, lizards, frogs, and insects.

BREEDING: 1 or 2 litters of 1–10 young are born between spring and late summer after a 34–37 day gestation. The young open their eyes after 30 days, wean at 6–7 weeks and sometimes breed as early as 3 months. Weasels rarely live longer than 1 year.

LIFESTYLE: Common weasels are solitary animals. Apart from mothers with young families they live alone, coming together only briefly to breed. Males play no part in the rearing of their young.
Notwithstanding their small size, weasels are phenomenal hunters.

They are incredibly quick and agile and can climb and swim well. Their active lifestyle burns a lot of fuel and weasels must eat half their own body weight in food every day.

They specialize in catching rodents and their sinuous body is well adapted to squeezing into narrow burrows. Their acute senses of sight, smell, and hearing detect prey or danger and they are amazingly strong, overwhelming animals larger than themselves with apparent ease. Prey is dispatched with a quick bite to the neck and may be carried several hundred meters to a safe eating-place. Weasels can hunt even under deep snow. When their prey of burrow-dwelling mice, voles, and rabbits is plentiful, weasels will kill as many prey as possible – more than they can eat immediately – and they will then store the surplus in a safe place as a precaution against winter shortages. When angered or alarmed, the weasel will produce a strong smell from glands at the base of the tail.

STAND TALL
Weasels often stand tall on their hind legs to scan their surroundings for the tell tale signs of potential prey.

AMERICAN MINK

> *Mustela vison*
> Family: MUSTELIDAE
> Order: CARNIVORA

DISTRIBUTION: Wetland areas throughout Canada and eastern and central USA. Introduced populations are well established in Britain, Iceland, France, Spain, Italy, and Scandinavia – the result of escapes and deliberate releases from fur farms.

SIZE: Length 12–18.5in (30–47cm); tail 5–9in (13–23cm); weight 1.1–4 lb (0.5–1.8kg). Males are larger than females.

APPEARANCE: A smart, sinuously attractive animal with a long body, short legs and a long, tapering tail. The head is small and neat with a pointed muzzle. The coat is dark brown, luxuriantly thick and glossy with creamy white markings on the chest.

DIET: Fish, frogs, small mammals, water birds, their eggs and young.

BREEDING: Mink breed once a year. Females produce litters of 4–6 young in a waterside den in April or May after a gestation period lasting 39–78 days including up to a month's delayed implantation (a period of dormancy before mother and embryo are linked via blood vessels). The young are weaned at about 5–6 weeks old and disperse soon afterwards. Providing they find a suitable territory, they are ready to breed at 11 months old. Longevity is about 10 years.

LIFESTYLE: Mink are solitary nocturnal predators. They live on the banks of rivers and lakes and mark out territories with heaps of very smelly black droppings. There may be several different dens within a territory; sometimes in abandoned burrows made by other animals, or tucked away in rock crevices or log piles. Young mink disperse away from their mother's territory on reaching independence but once settled, individuals may occupy the same territory their

FAVORED FUR
The American mink has been trapped for centuries for its dense fur. Fur farmers prefer this species to the European mink because of its hardiness and its color range.

entire adult lives. Male territories often overlap those of one or more females, with whom they may breed, but they do not participate in the rearing of young.

Mink appear lively and energetic. On land they run with sprightly grace, investigating every potential feeding opportunity but rarely pausing for more than a few seconds. They are equally at home in water, where they swim using their broad tail for propulsion and their feet to steer. In fact all this vigorous activity takes up only a small part of the mink's day and most animals spend up to 20 hours a day in their den. Mink devote long periods of time to grooming their magnificent fur – dense, glossy, and extremely warm. The fur industry exploits this species intensively.

KINKAJOU

Potos flavus
Family: PROCYONIDAE
Order: CARNIVORA

DISTRIBUTION: Tropical forests of Central America and northeastern South America.

SIZE: Length 16–30in (40.5–76cm); tail 15–22in (39–57cm); weight 3–10lb (1.4–4.6kg).

APPEARANCE: A lithe-bodied animal, with a long, prehensile tail and a small, round head. The face has large, forward-facing eyes and small, round ears on the sides of the head. The feet are strong, with five long-clawed fingers and toes on each. The coat is thick and velvety and usually some shade of tawny brown, sometimes with a black stripe down the back.

DIET: Fruit, insects and other small invertebrates, honey.

BREEDING: Kinkajous nest in hollow trees and females usually have just one young at a time. Gestation is 114–120 days and the young are born quite well advanced. They are weaned and able to climb by 7 weeks old, but do not breed until well into their second or third year. Longevity is up to 30 years.

LIFESTYLE: Kinkajous live alone except for mothers with young and courting pairs, which may associate for a few days. Both males and females are territorial and can be aggressive toward others of their own sex, but generally they just avoid each other by using loud, wailing calls and scent marks to make sure neighboring animals know they are around. An individual home range is anything up to 100 acres (40ha), and kinkajous will travel far each night looking for trees with ripe fruit or other good food. On average males travel almost twice as far as females. They hardly every come down to the ground and normally move carefully from branch to branch, making sure they are firmly anchored by the tail before committing their weight to a new branch. The feet are well adapted for climbing, despite the lack of opposable thumbs or toes. The pads are flexible and can grip the bark of trees.

KEEN SIGHT
Kinkajous are nocturnal. They have good night vision and their forward-facing eyes allow them to see in 3D and to judge distances.

EUROPEAN RIVER OTTER

Lutra lutra
Family: MUSTELIDAE
Order: CARNIVORA

DISTRIBUTION: Widespread but patchy across Europe and Asia from Great Britain to China and Korea. Hunting and pollution have caused local extinctions in many parts of the former range.

SIZE: Length 21–39in (60–95cm); tail 14–18.5in (36–47cm); weight 13.5–37.5lb (6–17kg). Males slightly larger than females.

APPEARANCE: This otter has a long slim body, with short legs, a long tapering tail and webbed feet. The muzzle is broad, the eyes and ears are small. The chestnut to dark brown fur is waterproof and incredibly dense, the throat, chest, and belly are creamy white.

DIET: Eats mainly fish, (especially eels) but also frogs, crayfish, mollusks, and other aquatic invertebrates.

BREEDING: Young adults reach sexual maturity at one year old. Litters of 2–4 young are born after 2 months gestation and raised by the females in a riverside den called a "holt" in the riverbank or under tree roots. Breeding is only seasonal in the north of the species range. Average lifespan is 3–4 years, but fortunate individuals may live 8 or 9 years.

LIFESTYLE: Otters are semi-aquatic and are equally at home in water or on land. Most hunting is done in water, where the otter swims with agile grace, using its webbed feet and sideways sweeps of its tail. Food is brought to the bank to eat. Hunting, like most otter activities happens mainly at night. Mature otters maintain territories along riverbanks, from which other adults of the same sex are excluded. Even as adults, otters can be playful animals; they seem to relish sliding down muddy banks, or on snow-covered slopes, and chasing in and out of the water. They tuck their legs back to gain speed and create the effect of a headlong "bellyflop" into the water.

WATERPROOF COAT
Underneath an outer coat of long, water-proofed hair, the otter has a thick layer of underfur that traps tiny air bubbles and helps keep the animal warm in and out of the water.

SEA OTTER

Enhydra lutris
Family: MUSTELIDAE
Order: CARNIVORA

DISTRIBUTION: Sea otters once ranged along Pacific coasts from California to Kamchatka and Japan but were hunted to extinction in much of this range. Reintroduced populations now thrive again between Alaska and California. The species favors kelp beds and rocky sea shores.

SIZE: Length 30–36in (75–90cm); tail 11–13in (28–32cm); weight 30–85lb (14–40kg).

APPEARANCE: Long-bodied and streamlined with short legs, completely webbed feet, and blunt-looking head. Rich brown coat fades to cream on the head with age.

DIET: Crabs, shellfish, sea urchins, fish, and other marine animals.

BREEDING: One pup is born each year after a period of development that can vary from 4 to 12 months. The delay ensures most cubs arrive in early summer regardless of when the mother mated.

LIFESTYLE: Sea otters are usually solitary animals, but sometimes gather into small groups. Males are territorial but animals of both sexes sometimes leave home and journey

100 miles (150km) or more along the coast before settling again. They spend a good deal of time grooming, to maintain the waterproofing and insulation of their magnificent coat. The incredibly dense fur allows it to spend longer swimming in cold water than any other mammal of equivalent size. But it is also the reason it cannot dive deeply or for longer than one minute – the air trapped among the hairs makes the otter very buoyant.

LAID BACK
Sea otters spend long periods drifting quietly and even dozing while floating on their back. They anchor themselves by draping a long strap of kelp across the chest to prevent them drifting too far in their sleep. They will carry their young on their chest and even crack open shells using a stone in this position.

EURASIAN BADGER

Meles meles
Family: MUSTELIDAE
Order: CARNIVORA

DISTRIBUTION: Most of Europe except northern Scandinavia, through the Middle East and Asia to Japan and southern China.

SIZE: Length 22–35in (56–90cm); tail 4.5–8in (11–20cm); weight 22–66lb (10–30kg).

APPEARANCE: A powerfully built, short-legged animal with grizzled, gray fur over most of the body. The face is long with small eyes and ears and a large black nose. The fur of the face is white with 2 broad black stripes running from the ears to the nose over the eyes. The feet are large with long, sharp claws.

DIET: Worms, insect larvae, slugs, and other invertebrates; also small mammals, amphibians, reptiles, birds and their eggs, fruit, fungi, roots, and carrion.

BREEDING: Gestation lasts 2 months and litters comprise 2–6 cubs, which are suckled for 11–12 weeks and reach sexual maturity at the end of their first year. Longevity is 12–14 years.

LIFESTYLE: Badgers are primarily nocturnal but on summer evenings they emerge from their underground sets (burrows) well before dark. Sets are used by generations of badgers and older sets can be very extensive. Badgers are fastidiously clean animals, and regularly empty the nest chambers of bedding materials. Soiled hay is dumped outside the set and fresh material is collected from nearby.

Badgers live communally, in extended family groups. Adult females mate with more than one male and cubs from the same litter may have different fathers. The young are playful and much more agile than the adults. From time to time mature adults will disperse away from the colony, joining another elsewhere or finding a mate and starting a new group. The ranges of neighboring groups overlap, but the area around the set is defended as a territory.

SLOWING DOWN
Badgers do not hibernate but they are generally less active in winter and bad weather can force them to stay indoors for several days at a time.

HOODED SKUNK

Mephitis macroura
Family: MUSTELIDAE
Order: CARNIVORA

DISTRIBUTION: Woodland, grassland, and desert from Arizona and southwest Texas to Costa Rica.

SIZE: Length 11–15in (28–38cm); tail 7–17in (18.5–43.5cm); weight 1.5–5.5lb (0.7–2.5kg). Males are larger than females, but generally have a shorter tail.

APPEARANCE: A lithe, brush-tailed animal with a small head, short legs and prominent claws. The coat is black with striking white stripes on the back and white markings on the head and flanks. The white areas have black hairs mixed with them; there may be a faint white stripe on each flank and a white stripe on the snout. Some animals have a black head.

DIET: Mainly insects and other invertebrates, plus small mammals, birds, eggs, carrion, plant material and garbage. Prey is ambushed or dug up rather than chased. Skunks are valuable predators of mice, rats, and insects, but may sometimes attack poultry, and are reported to carry rabies.

BREEDING: Courtship and mating happen in February and litters of 1–10 young are born in May. Weaning age is 8–10 weeks and the young leave their mother in the fall. Skunks breed at 1 year old. Their lifespan is about 8 years.

LIFESTYLE: The Latin name *Mephitis* means "foul smelling". When

threatened, the skunk can squirt a jet of evil-smelling sulphurous chemicals at its attacker. Hooded skunks occupy overlapping home ranges but normally avoid contact with one another. They den in hollow logs, rock piles and the underground burrows of other animals. Hooded skunks are most active between dusk and dawn. They do not hibernate but will sit out bad winter weather in their dens.

DANGER AND SAFETY SIGNALS
The skunk's striking black and white markings are a signal, warning other animals not to approach too closely. However, for skunks themselves, the pungent aroma is the smell of safety and recognition.

COMMON PALM CIVET

Paradoxurus hermaphroditus
Family: VIVERRIDAE
Order: CARNIVORA

DISTRIBUTION: Forests and wooded areas from India and Sri Lanka to Southeastern China and the Malay Peninsula, Sumatra, Java, Borneo, Sulawesi, the Philippines, and on many Southeast Asian islands. Often where humans dwell.

SIZE: Length 17–29in (43–71cm); tail 16–26in (41–60cm); weight 5.9–9.8lb (2.7–4.5kg).

APPEARANCE: A slim, short-legged animal with a long tail (not quite as long as its body length) and small head with pointed snout. The coat is buff to dark brown with black stripes down the back and spots on shoulders, flanks, and face; and there is a streak on the forehead. The face markings are mask-like. There are usually small to medium spots on sides and base of tail and the tip of the tail is sometimes white. Males and females are difficult to tell apart, hence the scientific name *hermaphroditus* (referring to species with both male and female reproductive organs).

DIET: Small vertebrates, insects, fruits, seeds, and plant exudates (sap and gum) – the species gets is alternative name "toddy cat" because of its liking for sweet palm sap, which can ferment to form an alcoholic "toddy."

BREEDING: Litters of 2–5 young are born at any time of year after a 2-month gestation period. Young civets are sexually mature at 12 months old and may live for up to 25 years in captivity, though usually much less in the wild.

LIFESTYLE: Common palm civets are expert climbers, using their sharp claws to grip tree trunks and branches and balancing with their long tail. This species, however, tends to spend more time foraging at ground level than other civet species. They are strictly nocturnal and by day each sleeps in its own personal tree, usually a palm or mango.

CAT RELATIVE
Civets, along with genets, are relatives of the cat family and have cat-like slim bodies and short legs. Being agile and inquisitive they sometimes get into human homes...
and lots of trouble.

Palm civets are solitary and territorial. Males defend territories of around 4 square miles (10sq km) from other active males, patrolling regularly and leaving scent marks. They will however tolerate the presence of immature and elderly males who do not threaten their supremacy or challenge their right to mate with local females. Females permit males within the periphery of their home range but not within the core area except in the breeding season. Civets are common in plantations and also in towns where they are sometimes encouraged because they catch and eat rodents. However civets can create a nuisance, stealing poultry, raiding fruit crops, and helping themselves to sap being tapped to make palm toddy. They eat a lot of fruit from palms but also from many other types of trees. Civets often set up home in houses, building dens in drainpipes and roof spaces and emerging at night to find food left by people.

COMMON GENET

Genetta genetta
Family: VIVERRIDAE
Order: CARNIVORA

DISTRIBUTION: Widespread and common in dense scrub, woodland, and rocky areas throughout Palestine and north Africa, the species also occurs in southern France and on the Iberian Peninsula.

SIZE: Length 16–21.5in (40–55cm); height 7–8in (18–20cm); tail 16–20in (40–50cm); weight 3–5lb (1.3–2.25kg).

APPEARANCE: A long, slim catlike animal with short legs. The coat is sandy colored with dark spots forming long stripes along the back and there is a crest of dark hair down the spine. The tail has 9–10 dark rings and a white tip.

DIET: Genets are opportunist hunters, eating most of whatever is available at the time. Common prey animals include rodents, especially mice, also baby rabbits, lizards, and birds, especially nestlings in spring and summer. They will also take and eat insects, and seasonal fruits and berries.

BREEDING: Genets can breed twice a year, and births peak around April–May and August–September. Litters of 1–4 young are born blind and helpless after a 70-day gestation period, but develop rapidly. By 8 weeks old they are ready to accompany their mother out of the nursery den (usually in a tree hole). By 6 months they are fully weaned and they become sexually mature at about two years old. They may live up to 20 years in captivity, but usually much less in the wild.

LIFESTYLE: Common genets are nocturnal – active at dawn, dusk, and during most of the night. They are skillful climbers and hunt in trees as well as on the ground. By day they make use of convenient tree hollows, rock crevices, or burrows to hide away and sleep, but they have no permanent den. Individual adults live alone, except during the breeding season when

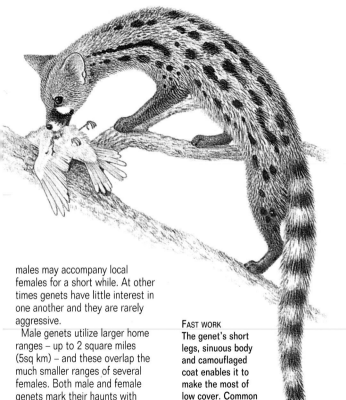

males may accompany local females for a short while. At other times genets have little interest in one another and they are rarely aggressive.

Male genets utilize larger home ranges – up to 2 square miles (5sq km) – and these overlap the much smaller ranges of several females. Both male and female genets mark their haunts with scent and use shared latrines. By visiting a well-marked spot, each genet can learn up-to-date information about its neighbors.

FAST WORK
The genet's short legs, sinuous body and camouflaged coat enables it to make the most of low cover. Common genets may have been imported to Europe by the Moors in the Middle Ages.

MEERKAT

Suricata suricatta
Family: HERPESTIDAE
Order: CARNIVORA

DISTRIBUTION: Southern Africa in Angola, Namibia, South Africa and South Botswana on dry savanna (or *veldt* as it is called in South Africa), open plains and scrubland.

SIZE: Length 12–18in (30–45cm); tail 6–12in (15–30cm); weight 3.3–5lb (1.5–2.25kg). Females are often larger than males.

APPEARANCE: A slim, long-bodied, short-legged animal, with a slender tail and tan to gray fur. There are dark markings on the back, flanks, ears and tail tip and around the eyes. They look rather like mongooses to whom they are related.

DIET: A wide range of foods including insects, scorpions and grubs; occasionally lizards, small snakes, birds, and mice. Foraging is a communal activity.

BREEDING: 2–5 young are born at any time of year after a 75-day gestation. They wean at 3–4 weeks and are sexually mature at about 12 months. Meerkats live up to 10 years.

LIFESTYLE: Meerkats are highly sociable. A pack may include several breeding pairs and there is no obvious hierarchy. Some females produce milk to suckle pack babies even if they have not been pregnant. Toward the end of weaning, young meerkats follow the pack on foraging trips and adults share the best food they find with their young apprentices. If a member of the pack is left injured it may be nursed back to health by the other members.

Meerkats are excellent diggers. Their warrens have many chambers and entrances and provide refuge from predators and a shelter from extremes of heat and cold. The territory of a meerkat pack may be up to 6 square miles (15sq km) and will

contain five or six warrens, which are occupied in turn. Males perform the job of marking of territories using scent from the anal glands, but all members of the pack help defend the territory and will fight with intruding packs. As with other mongooses, meerkats will stand on their hind legs to give themselves the best possible view for potential dangers on the horizon. At the first sign of danger, the "sentry" barks out a warning giving the rest of group time to disappear into the relative safety of their burrows.

ON THE LOOKOUT
All members of a meerkat pack perform their share of chores including baby-sitting, tunnel maintenance, and sentry duty, seen here. Meerkats have excellent vision and predators are nearly always spotted in time to alert the whole pack.

SPOTTED HYENA

Crocuta crocuta
Family: HYAENIDAE
Order: CARNIVORA

DISTRIBUTION: Grassland and open country south of the Sahara desert, excluding the Congo Basin. Population and range have declined due largely to human persecution.

SIZE: Length 3.1–5.4ft (0.95–1.66m); height 31–36in (79–91cm); tail 10–14in (25–36cm); weight 88–190lb (48–75kg). Females are larger than males.

APPEARANCE: Superficially doglike animal with short hind legs and sloping back. The muzzle is short and powerful, the yellow-brown coat is shaggy and rough with dark brown oval spots. The tail has a tuft of long dark hairs.

DIET: Any medium-sized hoofed mammals, especially wildebeest (mainly very young or very old animals) and carrion.

BREEDING: 1–3 young are born in den after a gestation of about 110 days. They are fully weaned at 12–16 months. Males reach sexual maturity at 2 years, females at 3 years. Captive individuals have lived for more than 40 years, but longevity in the wild is less.

LIFESTYLE: Hyenas waste nothing and will consume entire carcasses including bones, horns, and teeth. They often scavenge the remains of carcasses left by other predators. However they are also effective hunters, both in packs and alone.

Hyena social life is highly unusual. They live in large groups ("clans") of up to 80 animals, subdivided into smaller groups, dominated by females. But unlike wolf packs and lion prides there is little cooperation and the association is an uneasy one. Members of a clan behave aggressively to one another, especially where food is concerned. Hunting is the only activity with any real teamwork, and squabbles break out as soon as a kill is made. Their numbers have declined and the species is already extinct in parts of Africa.

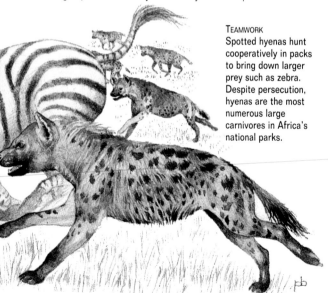

TEAMWORK
Spotted hyenas hunt cooperatively in packs to bring down larger prey such as zebra. Despite persecution, hyenas are the most numerous large carnivores in Africa's national parks.

KILLER WHALE

Orcinus orca
Family: DELPHINIDAE
Order: CETACEA

DISTRIBUTION: Found in all oceans and adjoining seas worldwide, from the poles to the tropics.

SIZE: The largest member of the dolphin family; length 21–26ft (6.5–8m); weight 2.5–8.85 tons (2.5–9 tonnes). Males usually about half as big again as females.

APPEARANCE: A huge, robust dolphin with broad pectoral fins and tail flukes and a tall dorsal fin. The body is jet black with white patches on the belly, chin and throat and behind the eye; there is also an indistinct gray saddle just behind the dorsal fin. The dorsal fin is erect, triangular, and up to 6 feet (1.8m) high, smaller and backwardly curved in female. Pectoral and tail flukes broad.

DIET: Fish, squid, turtles, penguins, and other sea mammals including seals and other whales. Orcas very often hunt in packs, driving shoals of fish or harrying larger whales, especially females with young, to the point of exhaustion before going in for the kill with their 50 or so large sharp teeth. When chasing prey they can reach speeds of 30mph (50kmh).

BREEDING: Calves are born singly at any time of year after a gestation of 16–17 months. They are suckled for up to 2 years although they begin taking solid food long before this. Males may live up to 60 years, females up to 90 years.

LIFESTYLE: Killer whales, or orcas, are highly social, and most live in pods of between 2 and 60 animals. These pods are led by a large male; these pods occasionally coalesce into larger schools of up to 250 animals. Only adult males live alone. Large pods tend to comprise one or more groups of related individuals, usually a mature female and her offspring, and sometimes several generations of the same

DORSAL I.D.
All killer whales are born with a tall, curved dorsal fin with smooth edges. Over time the fin accumulates various nicks and or scars, which help zoologists identify different individuals.

family. The members of a pod are protective of each other and young orphans may even be "adopted" by older relations. The strong social bond between killer whales sometimes leads to mass strandings, where whole groups become beached rather than abandoning an individual in distress.

Orca pods can be "resident" or "transient". Resident populations remain within a certain area all year around and can grow very large in areas where food is plentiful. Transient pods tend to be smaller and roam further afield. Different pods develop hunting traditions, specializing in certain kinds of prey.

Killer whales appear playful. They are very acrobatic and inquisitive, sometimes leaping clean out of the water or floating with their head above the waves to get a good look around. These antics make them popular with whale watchers and the species is probably the best known and loved of all cetaceans.

BOTTLE-NOSED DOLPHIN

Tursiops truncatus
Family: DELPHINIDAE
Order: CETACEA

DISTRIBUTION: Widespread in temperate and tropical open and coastal waters of the Atlantic, Pacific, and Indian Oceans and adjoining seas. The dolphins in the Pacific and Indian Oceans are sometimes regarded as a separate species to those in the Atlantic. They swim in open water, bays, lagoons, and reefs. Individuals will sometimes venture up estuaries and large rivers.

SIZE: Length 7.5–12.5ft (2.3–3.8m); weight: 330–1,436lb (150–650kg). Males are slightly larger than females, and members of offshore populations in higher latitudes tend to be heavier than those along tropical coasts. The distinctive "beak" is about 3.2in (8cm) long, and is said to resemble the top of an old-fashioned gin bottle – hence the dolphin's name.

APPEARANCE: A robust dolphin with a broad head and body, narrow beak, and rounded forehead. Body color usually dark

gray on the back, paler gray on the flanks and white or even pale pink on the belly. Older animals often spotted, especially on the belly.

DIET: Wide-ranging, including fish, squid, octopus, and other mollusks mostly caught on the bottom.

BREEDING: A single calf is born after a gestation period of about a year, and is suckled for as long as 4 to 5 years until the mother has another calf. Males reach sexual maturity at 10 to 12 years, and females at 5 to 12 years.

LIFESTYLE: Dolphins do not need to go deep to catch their food and most dives are between 10 and 150 feet (3–46m). In exceptional circumstances, however, they are capable of going up to 10 times deeper. Most prey is detected using underwater echolocation or "sonar". The dolphin's large brain analyzes individual echoes that the

HIGH JUMP
Bottle-nosed dolphins
are very acrobatic
animals and can leap
anything up to 30 feet
(9m) out of the water.
Young dolphins often
pick up "toys" such as
seaweed, sponges, or
jellyfish, with which
they play catching and
chasing games.

human brain could not separate
from background noise. Other
sounds, mainly clicks and squeaks,
are used for communication.
Bottlenoses generally live in casual
groups of anything from a half
dozen to 100 or more. Newly
independent dolphins live in
adolescent gangs. Sexually mature
females eventually mate and
graduate to nursery groups
comprising other mothers that help
each other to give birth and rear
young, while mature males remain
in small bachelor bands.

COMMON DOLPHIN

Delphinus delphis
Family: DELPHINIDAE
Order: CETACEA

DISTRIBUTION: Pacific and North Atlantic Oceans and all adjoining seas worldwide in tropical, subtropical and warm temperate waters. Common dolphins are usually found well out to sea.

SIZE: Length 59–102in (1.5–2.6m); dorsal fin 16in (40cm); weight 130–300lb (60–136kg).

APPEARANCE: A torpedo-shaped body with a rigid, backward curving dorsal fin. The snout is narrow and pointed, like a beak. The coloration is variable, usually brownish-black on the back and upper flanks; the underparts are creamy-white to white; the flanks have an hourglass pattern of tan or yellowish-tan, becoming paler and gray behind the dorsal fin, where it may extend to the dorsal surface. There is a black stripe from the flipper to the middle of the lower jaw and from the eye to the base of the beak. The flippers are black to light gray or white. In some animals there may be one or two gray lines running longitudinally along the lower flanks.

DIET: Squid and small fish.

BREEDING: Females breed once every 2–3 years from the age of 3–12 years (the wide variation reflects regional differences in competition and feeding resources). Gestation lasts 9–11 months and the calf is suckled for about 6 months. Potential longevity is 20 years or more.

LIFESTYLE: Common dolphins are among the most gregarious of all cetaceans. They live in huge schools, which routinely comprise 1,000 individuals and sometimes come together in mega schools a quarter of a million or more strong. Late in the day these schools break up into smaller hunting parties, but they regroup again at dawn and travel together by day. Members of these smaller subgroups are cooperative and appear to look

after one another. Wounded individuals and females in labor are helped by their companions to the surface to breathe.

In summer, schools of common dolphins spend more time a long way offshore and large concentrations develop in the north where long hours of daylight promote good feeding conditions. In winter they move toward the tropics and are more inclined to enter coastal waters.

RIDING THE WAVES
Dolphin schools swim fast, up to 25mph (40kmh), and often ride the bow waves of boats. They take long, low leaps out of the water – known as porpoising. As they swim they communicate using whistles and squeals. The clicking sounds so often associated with dolphins are used for echolocation.

BELUGA

Delphinapterus leucas
Family: MONODONTIDAE
Order: CETACEA

DISTRIBUTION: Coastal Arctic and sub-Arctic waters around North America, Greenland, Scandinavia and Russia. Some populations migrate regularly between feeding grounds and breeding areas and to avoid the build up of sea ice in winter.

SIZE: Length 10–21ft (3–6.5m); weight 1,100–3,300lb (500–1500kg). Males are longer and much heavier than females.

APPEARANCE: A chubby whale with no dorsal fin, a flexible neck and an expressive, blunt-snouted face with a round bulging forehead. The skin is creamy white and often scarred, that of young animals is slate gray to reddish brown and fades with age.

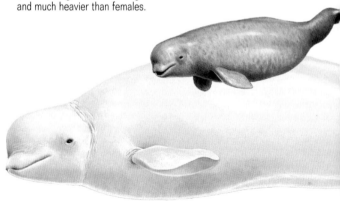

DIET: Schooling fish such as herring and cod, also crustaceans and squid.

BREEDING: Females mature at about 5 years, males at about 8. Calves are born one at a time after a 14-month gestation and may remain dependent on their mother's milk for up to 2 years. Individuals often live more than 25 years, sometimes as many as 40.

LIFESTYLE: Belugas along with Narwhals are so-called "white whales" and are among the most social of all cetaceans. They live in groups numbering anything from a dozen or so to several hundred. The largest aggregations form in summer when melting of ice around northern coasts allows the whales to come close to shore and even venture up river estuaries. They congregate in their hundreds and thousands at their birthing grounds in wide river estuaries. The species molts each summer and swimming in shallow water with a sandy bottom may help relieve itching as the old skin sloughs away. Belugas are very vocal, using a great variety of musical trills, squeaks, clicks, and whistles. They also communicate visually with a variety of facial expressions. No other whales have the facial muscles to do this.

CONSTANT CONTACT
The bond between mother and calf is very strong. The youngster takes advantage of its mother's slipstream to make swimming less arduous, and maintains almost constant contact with her. Young belugas often remain close to their mothers even after a new calf is born.

NARWHAL

Monodon monoceros
Family: MONODONTIDAE
Order: CETACEA

DISTRIBUTION: In summer narwhals frequent the deep waters of the Arctic Ocean. As the pack ice thickens in winter they retreat farther south and offshore into adjoining oceans and seas around North America, Greenland, Scandinavia and Russia.

SIZE: Length 10–15ft (3.0–4.7m); weight 0.8–1.5 tons (0.7–1.4 tonnes). Males are usually about half as big again as females.

APPEARANCE: A portly looking whale with a rounded head and tapering body. The pectoral fins are distinctive with upcurled edges but there is no dorsal fin. Males have a single, spiral-grooved tusk up to 8.6 feet (2.7m) long, protruding from snout. The color is mottled grayish-green, cream and black, whitening with age from the belly up; young dark gray. Juveniles are dark gray all over. The head is rounded, due to the pronounced forehead or "melon." The flippers curl upward and outward with age. The other teeth are not properly developed.

AN OVERGROWN TOOTH
The male narwhal's unique tusk is actually an overgrown tooth. The tooth is rooted in the upper jaw and grows outward, piercing the narwhal's lip when it is about 3 years old and continuing to grow throughout its life.

DIET: Bottom-dwelling fish such as flatfish, also squid, shrimps, crabs and other crustaceans.

BREEDING: A single calf is born in summer after a gestation period of about 15 months. The mother suckles it for at least a year and it has a life expectancy of up to 40 years.

LIFESTYLE: Narwhals are social and often gather in huge numbers, especially during the summer. Some groups are thought to contain many hundreds of whales, although such aggregations are temporary. The basic social unit is a group of between 5 and 20 individuals, but they may gather in larger schools to migrate. A procession of hundreds and even thousands of narwhals migrating along the coast is an amazing sight. Usually the group is all of one sex or one age group, as with pods of newly independent juveniles.

Mature males struggle for dominance and the right to mate, sometimes damaging their tusks in fights. In the Arctic Ocean, narwhals are dependent on cracks and holes in the ice for breathing. They sometimes break thin ice by ramming it with their heads – several narwhals may cooperate to break through the sea ice (using their melons) to make breathing holes. They are vulnerable to attacks by polar bears, which lie in wait at breathing holes. Narwhals are also prone to mass fatalities when shifting ice floes close off escape routes to the open sea.

SPERM WHALE

Physeter catodon Family: PHYSETERIDAE Order: CETACEA

DISTRIBUTION: Global; in all world's oceans and many adjoining seas but avoids polar waters. Spends most time in deep water, can dive to over 1.5 miles (2.5km), deeper than any other mammal.

SIZE: Length 11–19m (36–60ft) tail flukes up to 15ft (4.5m) wide; Weight: 16–55 tons (15-50 tonnes); males often twice as large as females.

APPEARANCE: Large, heavily built whale with dark blue-black skin often wrinkled and covered in scars with white markings around mouth; (color fades and becomes mottled with age). Vast, box-like head comprises up to one-third of body length. There is a single S-shaped blowhole on left hand side of snout. Body tapers strongly from head to tail. There is no dorsal fin. Males longer and up to 3 times heavier than females.

DIET: Sperm whales are the world's largest carnivores. They eat mostly squid, some octopus and fish, including sharks caught during deep dives.

BREEDING: Females reach breeding age at 8–13 years, males must wait up to 27 years to attain sufficient social status to breed. Mating happens mostly in spring and single young (calves) are born 14–16 months later in the fall of the following year. Calves are closely guarded by female and weaned at 2 years old or more. Potential longevity up to 77 years.

LIFESTYLE: The huge skull of the sperm whale contains the largest brain of any animal, but most of its volume is taken up by a mass of waxy material called spermaceti. When refined this produces oil of the highest grade, suitable for lubricating very fine machinery. This oil may help transmit high-frequency sounds for echolocation and communication, or it may help in buoyancy control. Another waxy substance, ambergris, is produced in the whale's gut. Ambergris was once valued highly by the perfume industry as a scent fixative. Today there are synthetic substitutes for spermaceti oil and ambergris, and hunting sperm whales was banned in the 1980s. The whale has up to 18 inches (35cm) of blubber to insulate it against the icy deep.

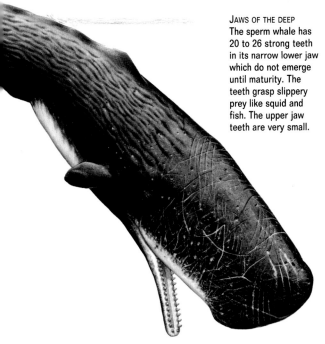

JAWS OF THE DEEP
The sperm whale has 20 to 26 strong teeth in its narrow lower jaw which do not emerge until maturity. The teeth grasp slippery prey like squid and fish. The upper jaw teeth are very small.

GRAY WHALE

Eschrichtius robustus
Family: ESCHRICHTIDAE
Order: CETACEA

DISTRIBUTION: Shallow coastal waters of Arctic and Pacific Oceans, from the Arctic Circle – Chukchi, Beaufort and Bering Seas and Sea of Okhotsk – south to Baja California and South Korea. Spends summer feeding in the Arctic, then migrates south to coastal bays and lagoons to breed. Hunting for meat and oil decimated the population in the past and the population breeding off Korea faces imminent extinction.

SIZE: Length 40–50ft (12–15m); weight: 16-39 tons (15-35 tonnes). Females are larger than males.

APPEARANCE: A large whale with a narrow head and large tail flukes. There is no dorsal fin, but along the middle of the lower back it has a row of small bumps or humps. There are 2 or 3 short curving throat furrows. The skin is dark, mottled gray and usually covered in patches of barnacles and whale lice.

DIET: Bottom-dwelling organisms, especially crustaceans; but also mollusks, worms, and small fish.

SLOW SWIMMER
The gray whale has a reasonably streamlined shape but is a slow swimmer. It grows to a maximum length of 50 feet (15m).

Food is sieved from the water using large plates of baleen (whalebone) hanging from the roof of the mouth.

BREEDING: Calves are born singly in warm water in winter after 13 months gestation. They begin feeding themselves at 7 months, become sexually mature at about 8 years and may live as long as 70 years.

LIFESTYLE: Gray whales are popular with whale watchers because they feed, breed and migrate close to shore. They are inquisitive, approach boats readily and indulge in antics such as breaching (leaping right out of the water), and spy-hopping (bobbing upright with the head out of the water).

These charismatic cetaceans make one of the longest annual mammal migrations in the animal kingdom. They travel up to 5,000 miles (8,000km) a year from the Arctic Circle to warm waters suitable for the birth of young. Migrating grays often travel in loose groups but they are generally less gregarious than some other species, spending long periods alone, especially when feeding. Mother gray whales migrating north with young travel quite slowly. There are also reports of other gray whales hanging back to support injured companions, even lifting them to the surface to breathe.

HUMPBACK WHALE

> *Megaptera novaeangliae*
> Family: BALAENOPTERIDAE
> Order: CETACEA

DISTRIBUTION: Worldwide in all oceans. Humpbacks spend most of their time in deep ocean but venture into shallower waters to breed.

SIZE: Length 36–50ft (11–15m); weight 33–44 tons (30–40 tonnes). Females are slightly larger than males.

APPEARANCE: A large dark gray to black whale with a tapering, knobby head and throat furrows extending all the way to the belly. The pectoral fins are very long (one third body length) with a variable white pattern on the underside. The tail flukes are also large and marked with white.

DIET: The humpback whale eats small shoaling fish and crustaceans, mainly krill. Squid and comb jellies (sea gooseberries) are also eaten. The furrows in the whale's throat allow it to expand enormously so that it can gulp huge quantities of food and water.

BREEDING: Females bear calves one at a time every other year in winter after 11.5 months gestation. Young whales are weaned at 11 months, reach breeding age after 4–6 years, and may live up to 77 years.

LIFESTYLE: Humpbacks belong to the Rorqual group of whales, which includes the giant Blue Whale, and means "furrow whale" (referring to the folds of skin below and behind the mouth). Humpbacks are one of the most vocal whales and their long, complex songs are hauntingly beautiful to the human ear. Only male humpbacks sing, in order to attract females and let other males know who is around. The "songs" are repeated sequences of sounds in complex patterns that can last for up to 35 minutes. The song is sung by solitary males during the breeding season, and varies from one population to another, a bit like human dialects. The songs evolve over time as whales copy variations

they hear. Humpbacks are filter feeders, but they also have some highly specialized feeding techniques. For example bubble-netting, in which fish are rounded up in a curtain of bubbles released from the blowhole. The whales circle the fish and drive them upwards, eventually trapping them at the surface and swallowing them in huge numbers. This species of whale is threatened as a result of overhunting; many whales also drown in fishing nets. In some areas they are in competition for food with commercial fishing boats.

BREACHED WHALE
This spectacular piece of behavior, where the whale lifts its body out of the water, is called "breaching." It makes them one of the most popular species for whale-watchers.

NORTHERN MINKE WHALE

Balaenoptera acutorostrata
Family: BALAENOPTERIDAE
Order: CETACEA

DISTRIBUTION: In all oceans of the Northern Hemisphere, usually in deep water just off the continental shelf and seldom more than 100 miles (160km) from land. Northern minkes spend the summer feeding in the Arctic Ocean and migrate to the tropics to breed in summer.

SIZE: The smallest of the rorqual whales (1 of 8 species of baleen whale). It grows to only about one-third of the size of the blue whale (also a rorqual). Length 26–36ft (8–11m); weight 6.5–11 tons (6–10 tonnes).

APPEARANCE: From the surface minkes are best recognized by the pointed snout and small dorsal fin set well back on the long, slim body. Unusually among large whales, they produce no obvious vapor "blow" when they surface to breathe. The skin is dark gray on the head and back, fading to white on the belly. The flippers are relatively short.

DIET: Krill, squid, and small fish.

BREEDING: Calves are born singly after 10–11 months gestation and weaned at 5 months. Current breeding rates are thought to be artificially high, as the species benefits from reduced competition for food due to over hunting of other large whales. Most females now breed every year and youngsters reach breeding age at just 6–8 years, as opposed to 12–13 years in the 1940s. Most minkes will have a life expectancy of up to 60 years.

LIFESTYLE: Minke whales are fast swimmers and being somewhat smaller than their cousins the blue, fin, sei, and Bryde's whales, are also more acrobatic. They are able to leap completely out of the water and often do so in the vicinity of ships, being apparently curious about people. Minkes are usually seen in pairs or small groups, but large aggregations are not uncommon, especially where there is a good source of food, or during migration. Individual whales communicate using a variety of vocalizations, and each whale appears to have its own signature call in the form of a unique sequence of low-pitched thudding sounds.

The northern minke feeds by straining quite large prey out of the water using 600 or so stout baleen plates hanging from the roof of its mouth. It takes larger prey than its close cousin the southern minke. Minke whales were saved from extinction by a worldwide ban in whaling in the 1980s. However some nations now wish to resume commercial whaling.

AT RISK
Since minkes are more abundant than other great whales they would be the first to be targeted should commercial whaling resume.

CALIFORNIA SEA LION

Zalophus californianus
Family: OTARIIDAE
Order: PINNIPEDIA

DISTRIBUTION: Rocky stretches of the Pacific coast of North America from California to British Columbia and also around the Galápagos Islands. Former Japanese population declined due to hunting for fur and is almost certainly extinct. Sea lions rarely venture more than 8 miles (13km) out to sea and haul out on land to rest and breed.

SIZE: Length 5–8ft (1.5–2.4m); weight 176–860lb (80–390kg). Males grow much bulkier and heavier than females.

APPEARANCE: The California sea lion is a typical eared seal, with a long neck and tapering body. The strong hind flippers can be used for walking on. Adult males have a high, domed forehead and dark brown fur, adult females are light brown, pups are almost black.

DIET: Mainly fish, especially mackerel and anchovies, along with the occasional squid.

BREEDING: Females bear one pup a year, in summer, after about 11 months of pregnancy. Mating takes place in shallow water about 3 weeks after pups are born. Pups nurse for 6 to 12 months. They can live for up to between 20 and 30 years.

LIFESTYLE: Sea lions are masters of the aquatic environment, and may spend up to 2 weeks at a time at sea. However they also spend long periods out of the water. Large numbers haul out on rocky shores and on floating jetties in harbors and lie packed together like sardines in a tin. In summer they are prone to overheating and must periodically cool off in the water. Minor squabbles break out as animals returning from the sea attempt to find a space in which to lie up. During the breeding season males establish beach territories of about 300 square feet (130sq m), containing a dozen or more females. Breeding colonies are very

noisy – males especially indulge in a lot of loud territorial barking and bellowing while patrolling their patch and driving off rivals. Though these sea lions are highly athletic, they are not particularly deep divers, and most food is caught in less than 100 ft (30 m) of water.

QUICK SWIMMERS
California sea lions can swim fast, up to 25mph (40kmh) or more.

WALRUS

Odobenus rosmarus
Family: ODOBENIDAE
Order: PINNIPEDIA

DISTRIBUTION: Along the edge of pack ice in the Arctic Circle and the northern reaches of the Atlantic and Pacific. Populations migrate south in winter and north in summer, following the Arctic ice and traveling up to 1,800 miles (3,000km) a year.

SIZE: Length 7.4–11.5ft (2.25–3.5m); weight 880–3,750lb (400–1700kg). Males are longer and more than twice as heavy as females. Pacific walruses are larger than those found in the Atlantic.

APPEARANCE: A huge, bloated-looking seal with two long white tusks, a bristly snout and broad front flippers. Body color ranges from pale tawny to cinnamon-brown and is darkest on the chest and belly. Immature animals are darker.

DIET: About 100lb (45kg) of mollusks, crabs, worms, other invertebrates and occasionally fish taken from the seabed each day.

The facial whiskers are used to sense prey hidden in soft sediments.

BREEDING: Walruses breed in large colonies and pups are born singly between April and June. Gestation lasts up to 16 months, but includes a period of delayed development that ensures the baby is not born too early in the season. The young may be suckled for up to 2 years. Females mature at 6–7 years, males at 8–10 years and maximum lifespan is more than 40 years.

LIFESTYLE: Outside the breeding season, male and female walruses rest in huge single sex groups, often several thousand strong. Communication is by means of loud bellowing, grunts and sometimes whistles – males are especially vocal. In summer, groups are smaller and comprise dominant males, females and newborn young.

Only the biggest, strongest males have an opportunity to mate. Fights regularly occur. Many males bear the scars of horrific tusk wounds in their thick skin. Walruses swim slowly using the hind flippers to propel themselves underwater. They rarely need to dive more than 100 feet (30m) deep to feed and most dives last less than 10 minutes. Although not endangered, their numbers were seriously reduced as a result of past hunting; and they are still poached today for their ivory tusks.

MULTI-USE TUSKS
The most distinctive feature of a walrus is its tusks. These are sometimes used in fighting, for helping the animal to haul itself out of the water, and for chipping away at the ice around breathing holes. However their main function is in display – good tusks indicate a healthy, high-ranking animal.

NORTHERN ELEPHANT SEAL

Mirounga angustirostris
Family: PHOCIDAE
Order: PINNIPEDIA

DISTRIBUTION: Cold coastal waters of the North Pacific; males venture as far north as the Aleutian chain, females range along coasts of Oregon and Washington. Breeding beaches are mostly on islands off California and Mexico.

SIZE: One of the world's largest seals; length 6.5–16.5ft (2–5m); weight: 1,300–6,000lb (600–2,720kg). Males are twice as long and three times heavier than females.

APPEARANCE: A huge seal with a dark gray-brown coat. Males have a floppy, inflatable nose and the pink, calloused skin of the chest is bald and often heavily scarred from fighting. Newborn pups are black, juveniles are silvery gray.

DIET: Deep-water and bottom-dwelling fish including slower moving fish such as small sharks, also squid and other invertebrates; often eats luminescent species that can be seen even in very deep dark water.

BREEDING: Single pups are born in winter after an 11-month gestation. Pups are suckled for 4 weeks, during which time they triple their body weight to more than 300lb (135kg). Females often lose half their own weight during the 2–3 months of the breeding season. Young seals mature at about 5 years old and live up to 20 years.

LIFESTYLE: Elephant seals live far out at sea for most of the time and come ashore twice a year, once in winter to breed and again in summer to molt. In between times they complete annual journeys of up to 12,000 miles (20,000km). The molting season sees groups of up to several hundred seals crowded on to beaches where they spend most of the time sleeping. Elephant seals molt not only their fur, but also the outer layer of skin. Six months later, they gather on shore again and bulls compete with one another for small territories on

which to set up harems of females and breed (a single male may mate with up to 80 females in a season). The bulls perform rearing and bellowing displays with their floppy nose inflated. If these do not establish dominance, physical combat may take place. Fights during which rivals crash together and rake each other's flesh with long canine teeth are not uncommon. Though not an endangered species, they became virtually extinct by overhunting during the last century.

DEEP AND DARK
Northern elephant seals remain at sea for 10 months of the year, and spend up to 90 percent of their time underwater. They dive deeper than any other seal – reaching depths of up to 5,000ft (1,500m) often catching prey at this great depth. Dives as deep as this last as long as 2 hours.

GRAY SEAL

Halichoerus grypus
Family: PHOCIDAE
Order: PINNIPEDIA

DISTRIBUTION: Spends much of the year offshore in the North Atlantic but breeds on rocky coasts of Britain, Scandinavia, Iceland, southern Greenland, Labrador, and Nova Scotia, and in the Inner Baltic Sea. The latter population is endangered by hunting and pollution.

SIZE: Largest member of the true seal family; length 83–130in (2.1–3.3m); weight 230–680lb (105–310 kg). Males can grow 2 to 3 times as big as females.

APPEARANCE: The coat is dark gray on the back, fading on the flanks to pale on the belly and marked all over with black spots and blotches. Males are often darker and more heavily spotted than females and their snouts are broad, conical, and longer, and body is generally heftier with more massive shoulders. Males also develop a heavy, scarred neck region. Both male and female also have large, peglike teeth.

DIET: Fish, especially cod and salmon, also halibut and herring, occasionally squid and octopus. Fishermen often claim that seals damage commercial fish stocks but there is no conclusive proof of this.

BREEDING: Pups are born singly in fall and early winter and weaned at 3–4 weeks of age, by which time they have tripled their birth weight. Young pups have almost white fur, called laguno, which molts to adult pelage after about 3 weeks. Females then mate once more. Females first breed at about 4 years old and generally live longer than males – up to 40 years.

LIFESTYLE: In the fall gray seals come ashore to breed at the same place every year. The oldest females appear first and their pups are born very soon after. The bulls arrive next and each one tries to establish a small group of females as his own exclusive harem. The

INQUISITIVE
Gray seals are very inquisitive animals and will hang in the water like this (below) to watch each other, boats, or observe what is happening on land. Their eyesight is quite poor.

biggest bulls and those that come ashore earliest have a big advantage, though their strength and energy dwindle over the ensuing weeks.

Outside the breeding season, gray seals haul out on rocks or sandbanks to rest, but spend most of their time at sea, sometimes traveling many hundreds of miles from their breeding beach.

Unlike sea lions, true seals cannot stand on their hind flippers. On land they are ungainly and must drag themselves along with their flippers. While at sea, however, they are supremely agile. They swim underwater, hunting and eating large quantities of a wide variety of fish. Their hind flippers help them steer and orientate in the water as well as helping to propel them on land.

HARP SEAL

Phoca groenlandica
Family: PHOCIDAE
Order: PINNIPEDIA

DISTRIBUTION: There are three harp seal populations and these breed on the edge of pack ice in Newfoundland, the Jan Mayen Islands, and the White Sea. All populations disperse northwards in summer, migrating 3,000 miles (5,000km) or more between breeding grounds and feeding areas.

SIZE: Among the smallest seal species. Length 5.4-6.2ft (1.65–1.9m); weight 250–310lb (115–140kg).

APPEARANCE: A relatively slender and active species, the adults are light gray or silvery-white with a black face and a bold harp-shaped marking on the back (mostly of males, some females never develop full harps and remain spotted). Newborn pups have silky white fur called "laguno."

DIET: Harp seals eat shrimps and small fish, especially capelin. Fisheries claim harp seals are at

least partly responsible for the decline in stocks of commercially important fish, especially Atlantic cod. But this claim is difficult to verify.

BREEDING: Both sexes mature at about 5.5 years, but usually do not breed until about 8 years old. Pups are born singly in February, and mating happens a few weeks later. Pups are suckled for just 12 days then abandoned. Life expectancy is up to 30 years.

LIFESTYLE: Harp seals breed on the Arctic ice but spend much of the year far out at sea where they can feed well. Most prey, such as shrimp and small fish, are caught near the surface in open water. However, adults may dive down to 500 feet (150m) to catch larger shoaling species such as herring and cod. The seals have large, sensitive eyes and hunt mainly by sight. They communicate above and below the water using up to 15 different vocalizations, including grunts and barking sounds. With the wailing of young pups, breeding areas can be especially noisy places. Harp seals swim fast underwater and adults can also move quite rapidly on the ice, using their front flippers to haul themselves over the slippery surface. Young pups are far less mobile, which makes them easy targets for human hunters who controversially dispatch them with clubs so as not to damage their valuable white coat.

The harp seal is also known as the Greenland (or saddleback) seal, as it is found on the drift ice around the Greenland coast.

LONG-DISTANCE SEAL
Harp seals may travel long distances from the open water using channels among the ice floes. Journeys of over 3,000 miles (5,000km) between feeding and breeding grounds are regular. When out of the water, they prefer areas of thick, hummocky ice, which offer some shelter from the wind and snow.

RUFFED LEMUR

> *Varecia variegata*
> Family: LEMURIDAE
> Order: PRIMATES

MADAGASCAR

DISTRIBUTION: Sparsely distributed in the rain and humid forests of northeastern Madagascar (the island on which all lemur species are found except for some introduced to the Comoro Islands to the northwest).

SIZE: Length 20–23in (51–60cm); tail 22–25in (56–65cm); weight 6.6–11lb (3.2–5kg).

APPEARANCE: A lithe-bodied primate with a long, thickly-furred tail and a neat pointed face. Color shows variable patterning in black-and-white, red-and-white, or brown-and-white. Subspecies are defined by these coat colorings. The fur is long, dense, and soft, with a ruff from ears to chin. The face is covered by short hair and the hands and feet are naked with dark skin.

DIET: Leaves and fruit taken from the upper strata of the rain forest.

BREEDING: Young are born in litters of 1–3 in a nest of twigs and leaves, after a gestation of 90–102 days. It is the only lemur known to leave its young in the nest. The breeding season is short and the female is only "in heat" for a single day.

LIFESTYLE: These rain forest inhabitants have not been as well studied as their best known relatives the ring-tailed lemurs; but what is known is that they are the largest of the lemurs and mostly active at dusk. They are good climbers and spend much of their life in trees. All lemur species live in small family groups or pairs (pair-living is rare among other primates, but not lemurs). Ruffed lemurs live in small groups and these can change on a daily basis, varying in size and composition.

BLACK AND WHITE
There are several
subspecies based on
coloration – this is
the black and white
variety making scent
markings.

However, normally there will be an equal number of male and female adult members. Male lemurs are the same size or smaller than females and do not have enlarged canines (as with other primates). Males are also submissive and female dominance is often displayed on males without aggression.

Lemurs are very vocal using calls to alert others to predators or to communicate using scent which is secreted from special scent glands located on the throat, hands, and anal area. Lemurs will groom each other, just like monkeys and apes. They use their lower incisors which are tilted forward at an angle of 45° to act as a specialized "toothcomb", helping to remove excess fur and parasites from their grooming partner. Most social interactions are casual, only mothers and young form any kind of lasting relationship.

DWARF BUSH BABY

Galagoides demidoff
Family: GALAGONIDAE
Order: PRIMATES

DISTRIBUTION: Forest and densely vegetated marginal land in tropical western and central Africa, especially among dense vines or lianas. 3 distinct populations: Senegal, southern Mali, Burkina Faso and southwest Nigeria; Congo, Dem. Republic of Congo, Uganda, Burundi, and western Tanzania; a small group along the coast from southern Somalia to northern Tanzania.

SIZE: The smallest primate in Africa; length 4–6in (10–15cm); tail 6–8in (15–21cm); weight 1.6–4.2oz (46–120g).

APPEARANCE: A tiny primate with a long, furry tail and a round face dominated by huge black eyes. Pale stripe between the eyes. Nose is short, upturned, and pointed; the ears rounded. Coat color ranges from gray-black to bright ginger with paler yellowish underparts.

DIET: Mainly small insects, also tree sap, fruits, and nectar.

BREEDING: Young are born singly or occasionally as twins, after a 110 to 114 day gestation. They are suckled by the mother for 2 months, and gain independence and sexual maturity at 8 to 9 months. Individuals have lived up to 12 years in captivity.

LIFESTYLE: Dwarf bush babies are nocturnal and spend the day sleeping in dense thickets, tree holes or nests woven from leaves and twigs. Males usually sleep alone but occasionally share a nest with a female. Females are sometimes found sleeping in groups of 6 or more. They are active for most of the night, foraging alone but keeping in constant voice contact with neighboring animals. Bush baby calls include loud chirps and buzzing alarm calls.

Male bush babies use home ranges of up to 2.5 acres (1ha). These overlap with the ranges of several females and, around the edges, with those of other males. Females are nonterritorial but aggressive encounters between large males are common. Small males, however, are often permitted to wander freely within the ranges of dominant animals, presumably because they are not perceived as serious rivals.

Young bush babies are born in a secure nest, but after a few days their mother carries her offspring with her when she goes out to feed. At five weeks old a youngster is mobile enough to follow its mother on short journeys, but it takes several months to develop the extraordinary agility required to move freely through the dense, tangled vegetation.

Dwarf bush babies are lively, agile, and capable of huge horizontal leaps. Their long hind limbs propel them, while their bushy tails provide balance when jumping.

GIANT LEAPS
A bush baby can leap 6.5 feet (2m) – an astounding feat for an animal little bigger than a mouse.

SLENDER LORIS

Loris tardigradus
Family: LORISIDAE
Order: PRIMATES

DISTRIBUTION: India and Sri Lanka from rainforest to dry, swampy or scrubby forests. The species is declining as a result of habitat loss caused by logging and human development in the area.

SIZE: Very small primate. Length 6–10in (16–26cm); weight 3–12.5oz (85–350g).

APPEARANCE: Slender-limbed, primate with short, woolly, gray fur. Unlike its relative, the bush baby, the slender loris has no tail. The face is short with a pink nose and huge round eyes surrounded by dark patches of fur. The feet and hands are adapted for grasping, with large opposable thumbs and big toes. Their fingers and toes are very flexible and have nails rather than claws.

DIET: Fruits, shoots, flowers, and leaves. They use their hands to pluck fruit and leaves. Also insects, occasionally birds' eggs, and small lizards.

BREEDING: 1 or 2 young are born in spring or fall after a gestation of 166–169 days. They are weaned between 2 and 7 months. Females mature faster and may breed at 10 months old, males later, at about 18 months. Lorises can live up to 15 years.

LIFESTYLE: With its dull gray fur and slow-moving arboreal way of life, the slender loris is an inconspicuous animal at the best of times. By day, when it is not hunting, it curls up in a ball to sleep. Its extreme caution allows it to creep very close to prey before grabbing it – indeed insects and other small invertebrates often approach the loris without realizing it is there.

When threatened with discovery the slender loris has the ability to freeze and remain motionless for hours at a time, making itself virtually invisible. This tactic works well in hiding it from casual

CLOWN FACE
The name *Loris* is from the Dutch for "clown". It refers to the primate's eye patches, fixed stare, and comically careful movements.

observers and animals that hunt mainly by sight, but the loris is also capable of moving at unexpected speed, and will drop to the ground and scuttle to safety if approached too closely. When unsure of itself it may also sway forward and back and from side to side as though drunk. These primates rarely jump.

Lorises are solitary and territorial. They mark their territory with scent in their urine and aggressively repel intruders of the same species. The slender loris and the related slow loris seem to be able to eat food that would be toxic to most animals, such as millipedes and certain ants.

The slender loris has a particularly mobile hip joint for climbing, which it does in a slow-moving fashion. Its four limbs are roughly equal in length and it moves on all fours.

COMMON MARMOSET

Callithrix jacchus
Family: CALLITRICHIDAE
Order: PRIMATES

DISTRIBUTION: Relatively common in coastal and riverside rain forest and many other forest habitats in northeastern Brazil. Introduced populations are doing well in other parts of South America.

SIZE: Length 4.5–6in (12–15cm); tail 12–14in (30–35cm); weight 10.5–12.5oz (300–360g).

APPEARANCE: A small monkey with a long gray- and white-banded tail. The fur is generally mottled grayish-brown, darker on the head, with a distinctive white forehead and long white ear tufts. The infants are more uniformly gray.

DIET: Eats mainly tree gums and sugary sap collected from wounds that it gouges into the bark with its lower incisors. It also eats fruits and other plant material supplemented with some small animal prey including insects, spiders, small lizards, frogs, bird's eggs, and nestlings. Prey is caught and manipulated with the hands.

BREEDING: Dominant females first breed at 14–24 months and can rear 2 litters of 1–4 young a year with the help of their mate and other marmoset helpers. Gestation lasts 130–150 days and young are weaned after 100 days. Longevity is about 10 years in the wild, 16 years in captivity.

LIFESTYLE: These adaptable little monkeys are active during the day. They live in groups of up to 15 individuals, with a home range of around 25–100 acres (10–40ha).

In each group of common marmosets the dominant animal is a breeding female. There can also be one or two dominant males, and the rest of the group comprises offspring, plus one or two unrelated individuals. The dominant female produces chemicals called pheromones that inhibit breeding in the other adult females in the group. Courtship is initiated by the female, who stares at one of her

male companions and performs a
lip-smacking, tongue-flicking
display, which he reciprocates.
Instead of breeding themselves,
subordinate females help care for
the young. Common marmosets
are very territorial monkeys.

KEEP OUT!
Common marmosets
patrol in troops defend-
ing their patches with
loud whistling calls and
by displaying their
rumps and conspicuous
white genitals.

COMMON SQUIRREL MONKEY

Saimiri sciureus
Family: CEBIDAE
Order: PRIMATES

DISTRIBUTION: Tropical forests of the northern Amazon Basin from Colombia to northeastern Brazil and south to Peru.

SIZE: Length 11–14.5in (28–37cm); tail 14.5–18in (37–45cm); weight 1.2–2.8lb (0.55–1.25kg). Males are very slightly larger than females.

APPEARANCE: A small, neat monkey with a very long tail, long limbs and long, slender fingers and toes. The face white with a neat black muzzle, close-set eyes and large, fluffy ears. The fur is gray-brown on the back, darker on the tail tip, paler on the chest and belly and reddish on the arms and legs.

DIET: Fruit, insects and other invertebrates.

BREEDING AND YOUNG: Young are born singly after a 170-day gestation. Females first breed at about 3 years old, males at about 5 years. Squirrel monkeys are quite long-lived – in good conditions they can reach 30 years old.

LIFESTYLE: Squirrel monkeys are among the most social New World primates. They usually live in groups of 20 to 50, though groups of several hundred have sometimes been reported in areas of pristine forest. Within these large troops are smaller social groups, comprising females with young and gangs of adult and adolescent males. During the breeding season the adult males fight for dominance and only the highest-ranking males get much opportunity to mate. Females with young are aggressive toward males. The monkeys are active by day, though they take a siesta around noon. Squirrel monkeys are extremely vocal. Zoologists have recorded more then 25 distinct calls, ranging from soft purring sounds to loud barks and piercing squeals. Common squirrel monkeys belong to the

capuchin group of monkeys of the
South American forest ("capuche"
refers to a monk's hood which the
monkey's cap of dark fur
resembles). Like other capuchin-
type monkeys, squirrel monkeys
spend most of their lives high up in
trees. They are extremely agile at
running along the branches. The
long tail is invaluable – it flicks
from side to side helping the
monkey keep its balance.

BALANCING ACT
Squirrel monkeys grip the
tree branches tightly with
their long fingers and
toes. The long tail hangs
loose and is used like a
tightrope walker's pole –
for balance only.

MANDRILL

Mandrillus sphinx
Family: CERCOPITHECIDAE
Order: PRIMATES

DISTRIBUTION: Evergreen coastal forests of equatorial West Africa. Many mandrills are threatened by deforestation and hunting, and the species is listed as Vulnerable.

SIZE: Length 22–37in (55–95cm); height 18–24in (45–60cm); tail 2–3in (5–8cm); weight 22–66lb (10–30kg). Males are on average almost twice as big as females.

APPEARANCE: A large, powerful baboon with olive-brown fur. Males have a large mane and a strikingly colored face, with a ridged blue and crimson muzzle and naked red-and blue-skinned rump patches. The colors are most vivid in dominant animals.

DIET: Mandrills eat mostly fruits, but these primates will also eat almost anything, including small animals. The diet also includes leaves, roots, fungi, land crabs, and snails. Sometimes they catch and kill lizards, mice, and even small antelope.

BREEDING: Females give birth to single offspring after 6 months gestation. The youngster receives devoted care for 2 years or more. Young mandrills reach puberty at about 4 years, but males spend many years working their way up the dominance hierarchy before they get the chance to breed.

LIFESTYLE: Most mandrills live in small troops of up to 30 animals, mostly adult females and young. The group is led by a single dominant male. There may be one or two subordinate males, tolerated by the leader as long as they do not challenge his authority.

Mandrills are active during the day. They are agile climbers and sleep in trees at night, but they feed mostly on the ground, moving from place to place as supplies are used up. Troops are noisy, and most activities are accompanied by vocalization, from soft grunts to squeals and barks.

BLUE IN THE FACE
There is no mistaking who
is boss in a mandrill troop.
The lead male's vivid facial
coloring makes him stand
out from the crowd, even in
the dense forest gloom.

OLIVE BABOON

Papio anubis
Family: CERCOPITHECIDAE
Order: PRIMATES

DISTRIBUTION: Savanna grassland and light woodland from Mali to Ethiopia, south to Tanzania and in mountainous areas within the Sahara Desert.

SIZE: Length 19.5–54.5in (0.5–1.14m); tail 17.5–28in (45–71cm); weight 24–110lb (11–50kg). Males are substantially bigger than females and often more then twice as heavy.

APPEARANCE: A long-legged monkey with a short tail and a long, doglike snout. Baboons usually move on all fours. The fur is olive-brown, becoming increasingly gray with age and mature males develop a mane of long, frizzy hair around the head and shoulders. The skin of the face is sparsely haired.

DIET: Mostly grass and fruit, also tree gum, sap, and insects, especially locusts.

BREEDING: Young are born singly after 6 months gestation and are weaned at 6–8 months of age. These primates can live to 45 years of age.

LIFESTYLE: Olive baboons live in troops of up to 200 individuals, though most groups comprise about 50. Members of a group use mutual grooming as a way of forming and maintaining social bonds; for example, often a female will exchange grooming services for the opportunity to handle another female's infant.

There will be several dominant males within a troop, and they compete with one another to mate with each female that comes into estrus ("in heat"). The females are related while the mature males, of lesser number, are unrelated. Olive baboons are diurnal

(active during the day) and will travel several miles each day in search of food. Movements are initiated by dominant males, but the troop is usually led by a younger male who scouts ahead and raises the alarm if he meets danger. When the troop rests, it may well subdivide into smaller subgroups. They sleep in trees or on cliff ledges.

VARIED DIET
Like other members of the baboon family, olive baboons primarily eat fruit. However, they are known to include a range of foods, such as small mammals, in their diet.

111

RHESUS MACAQUE

Macaca mulatta
Family: CERCOPITHECIDAE
Order: PRIMATES

DISTRIBUTION: From Afghanistan through India and Nepal to Indochina and southern China, in forests and marginal land, including towns and villages. Population once seriously depleted, but today receives better protection and numbers are recovering.

SIZE: Length 17.5–25in (45–640cm); tail 7.5–12.5in (19–32cm); weight 12–26.5lb (5.5–12kg). Males are larger than females.

APPEARANCE: A large monkey with brown fur, a long tail and a naked, red-skinned rump that has no swelling. Face and rump naked, red in adult. Paler underparts.

DIET: Mostly vegetable matter including shoots, fruits, seeds, roots, bark, sap and some crops. Will also eat invertebrates, birds and scraps of food left by people.

BREEDING: Most births result in just one young, born after a

gestation lasting 133–200 days. Older females carry their young for much longer than first time mothers. Young are weaned for about a year and are ready to breed themselves at 2–4 years. Longevity is about 30 years.

LIFESTYLE: Rhesus macaques live in large groups and are active by day. Members of a troop communicate using a wide range of calls. Females in particular form close associations and engage in social activities like mutual grooming. The monkeys are naturally tree dwellers, but they have taken very well to life in towns and villages. In areas of natural forest habitat population density rarely exceeds 130 per square mile (50 animals per sq km), but in cities such as Calcutta there may be more than 700 animals living in the same area, taking advantage of human habitation for shelter, stealing food from houses and traders or scavenging in the streets. They are tolerated because Hindus regard them as sacred animals. The so-called "rhesus factor", found in human blood, was discovered in rhesus monkey blood in 1940. The rhesus factor, which helps define blood types in humans, means that rhesus macaques are often taken to zoos and used in medical research.

SOCIAL GROUPS
Rhesus live in groups containing more females than males. Spare males tend to live alone.

PROBOSCIS MONKEY

Nasalis larvatus
Family: CERCOPITHECIDAE
Order: PRIMATES

DISTRIBUTION: Restricted to the island of Borneo (Indonesia and Malaysia). Freshwater mangrove and lowland rain forest. However, over half of Borneo's mangrove forest has been destroyed in the last few decades and the remainder is now more accessible to hunters, and logging and mining companies than ever before.

SIZE: Length 21–30in (53–76cm); tail 22–30in (56–76cm); weight: 17–30lb (7–22kg); adult male about twice the weight of female.

APPEARANCE: Large, thickset, red-faced with short neat fur, reddish brown on back, creamy white on belly and insides of arms and legs; feet partially webbed. Adult male has highly visible, elongated, tongue-shaped, drooping nose; this is small and snub in females and young. Long tail used for balancing.

DIET: Huge quantities of tough mangrove leaves, some of which are toxic to other animals. Digestion is assisted by special gut-dwelling bacteria. Diet is supplemented by fruit, seeds and flowers when available.

BREEDING: Breeding appears to happen at any time of year and young are born one at a time. The gestation period is 5.5 months. Newborn has vivid blue facial skin. Young are cared for by their mother and are weaned after about 7 months.

LIFESTYLE: These are the world's most aquatic primates. They are expert swimmers both under water and at the surface and can dive in from a height of 50 feet (15m) or more. They never venture far from water, preferring dense freshwater mangrove forest where the trees overhang the rivers, and the forest floor is often flooded. Most foraging is done in the trees, but the water is used for cooling off and as an emergency escape route.

BADGE OF SUCCESS
Only healthy male
proboscis monkeys
live long enough to
grow a really
big nose.

HANUMAN LANGUR

Semnopithecus entellus
Family: CERCOPITHECIDAE
Order: PRIMATES

DISTRIBUTION: The Indian sub-continent from southern Tibet to Sri Lanka and including parts of Nepal, Bhutan, Bangladesh, Afghanistan, Pakistan and India. Has declined severely due to habitat loss and is listed as endangered.

SIZE: Length 16–31in (41–78cm); tail 27–42.5in (0.69–1.08m); weight 12–52lb (5.4–23.6kg).

APPEARANCE: A slender, long-tailed monkey with fine, gray-brown fur and dark skin. The face, ears, palms and soles are hairless. The long tail is not a prehensile one.

DIET: Mostly leaves, but will also eat flowers, fruits and crops.

BREEDING: Females begin breeding at 3–4 years of age and can bear one baby (occasionally twins) every 15–24 months. Gestation lasts 190–210 days and there is no fixed breeding season. Young are weaned at about 12 months and may live well over 20 years.

LIFESTYLE: Langurs are highly social and where conditions suit them can live at very high densities. Most individuals live in large troops led by one or more adult males. Other males live in bachelor groups with a dominance hierarchy. Young males start low down on the ladder and fight their way towards the top in preparation for taking over a breeding troop. Having acquired a group of females, the new male often kills very young babies in order to bring the females into breeding condition sooner. Ousted troop leaders

usually live alone. Langur troops are non-territorial and the ranges of neighboring groups often overlap. Troops keep each other up to date on their whereabouts with a daily chorus of whooping, usually early in the morning. Some of the largest groups recorded number several hundred individuals and probably represent two or three troops that have come together to share a good source of food or other resource.

Although the Hanuman langur, like other langurs, has long fingers and toes ideally suited to climbing among the branches, it spends a lot of time at ground level. Like all Old World monkeys, Hanuman langurs have tough sitting pads on their bottoms.

WELL GROUNDED
Langurs are not as dependent on trees as other monkeys. This individual has come down to drink from a puddle, but some langurs do almost all their foraging at ground level. They are wary and alert to signs of danger.

BONOBO

Pan paniscus
Family: PONGIDAE
Order: PRIMATES

DISTRIBUTION: Lowland and swamp forest south of the Congo River in the Democratic Republic of Congo. This remote and restricted distribution is one reason the species was not recognized until 1929. Bonobos are endangered as a result of hunting and habitat loss.

SIZE: Height 28–33in (70–83cm); weight 68–86lb (31–39kg). Males are up to 30 percent bigger than females. Also known as the pygmy chimpanzee, the bonobo is not really any smaller than a regular chimpanzee.

APPEARANCE: This primate is slim and long-legged with dark brown to black fur and a dark-skinned face. The hair on the head is often rather tousled.

DIET: Mostly plant material, including fruit, leaves, seeds and flowers. Also some animal matter including various invertebrates and occasionally small mammals and snakes.

BREEDING: Babies are born singly at any time of year after around a 230 to 240-day gestation. Young are not weaned for 3 or 4 years and remain dependent on the mother even longer. Sexual maturity comes at about 7 years and maximum longevity is probably over 50 years.

LIFESTYLE: Bonobos live in social groups of 50 to 120 members, with the highest-ranking animals being female. Subgroups within the troop comprise an older female and her offspring. Each youngster receives up to seven years of individual care from its mother and young males will remain closely associated with her for life. Young females usually join another troop before breeding. Social bonds between all troop members are reinforced by mutual grooming – removing parasites from one another's coats. Gang fights between troops may break out if food is scarce.

BRANCH DWELLER
Bonobos sleep in the trees in specially constructed nests. They also do most of their foraging among the branches. On finding a new source of food, a bonobo summons other members of its troop with a loud call.

WESTERN GORILLA

Gorilla gorilla
Family: PONGIDAE
Order: PRIMATES

DISTRIBUTION: Tropical rain forest in parts of Cameroon, Central African Republic, Congo, Democratic Republic of Congo, Equatorial Guinea, and Gabon.

SIZE: Length 4.9–5.9ft (1.5–1.8m); standing upright with knees slightly bent 4.1–5.7ft (1.25–1.75m); weight 155–600lb (70–275kg). Males grow much bigger and heavier than females.

APPEARANCE: Huge ape with long, powerful arms and smaller legs, a broad chest and large head. The coat is brownish-black. The skin is jet black. When a male reaches maturity the hair on his back turns gray. This visible silvery white saddle extends down to the rump and gives rise to name "silverback" for dominant males in the group. There are two recognized subspecies: the Western lowland gorilla (*G. g. gorilla*) shows a distinctive red forehead, especially on the male; the Cross River gorilla (*G. g. diehli*) is Critically

Endangered and survives with just a few hundred individuals on the Nigeria-Cameroon border.

DIET: Fruit, shoots, leaves, bark, roots and bulbs.

BREEDING: A single baby is born after a 7–8 month gestation and remains dependent on the mother until weaned at 3–4 years. Males mature slower than females and individuals may live up to 50 years.

LIFESTYLE: The largest living primates, gorillas are peaceful, sociable creatures. They rarely act aggressively towards people, and even the chest-beating display of a dominant male is usually just a bluff. Both hands and feet have an opposable thumb or big toe for grasping branches.

Western gorillas live in smaller groups than eastern gorillas. They are also more mobile, an adaptation to a mainly fruit-eating diet.

A small group is more able to travel in search of trees with ripe fruit and less likely to run out of food before everyone has eaten their fill. They normally feed during the morning and afternoon, and rest for an hour or two around midday.

ON ALL FOURS
Gorillas can stand on two legs, but for everyday getting about they use all fours, walking on the soles of their feet and the knuckles of their hands. This is a Western lowland gorilla with its noticeable red forehead.

ORANG-UTAN

Pongo pygmaeus
Family: PONGIDAE
Order: PRIMATES

DISTRIBUTION: Once widespread in Southeast Asia and Indochina, now confined to the dwindling forests of Sumatra and Borneo.

SIZE: Length 31–38in (0.8–1m); standing on hind legs 3.7–4.5ft (1.15–1.4m); arm span around 7.3ft (2.2m); weight 66–200lb (30–90kg). Male orang-utans are up to twice as big as females.

APPEARANCE: An unmistakable large ape with very long, powerful arms and relatively short, weak legs. The coat is thin and shaggy and ranges from bright orange to maroon or dark brown. The palms, soles and face are naked. The face pinkish in young animals, black in adults. They are remarkable climbers – their feet look more like hands, with long digits and an opposable big toe.

DIET: Mainly fruit, especially figs and durians, also leaves, young shoots, bark, flowers, insects and occasionally birds' eggs.

BREEDING: A single baby (occasionally twins) is born at any time of year following a gestation period of 233–265 days. A young orang remains with its mother for several years. During that time it learns how to find and eat fruit among the trees and on the jungle floor. It walks on all fours and is weaned at 3–4 years. It reaches puberty at 7–10 years, though males rarely mate before their 14th year. Longevity can be up to 60 years. They are an endangered species because of habitat loss and past collection for zoos and as pets.

LIFESTYLE: Orang-utans live alone in the same home range for much of their adult life. They develop an intimate knowledge of the forest; which trees fruit when, which branches will bear their weight and how to get from one place to another more efficiently. They also know their neighbors, but avoid meeting up with them.

SOLITARY MALES
Adult male orang-utans develop large fleshy pads on either side of the face. Males rarely meet up, but when they do, aggressive displays and fighting may occur.

AFRICAN SAVANNA ELEPHANT

Loxodonta africana
Family: ELEPHANTIDAE
Order: PROBOSCIDEA

DISTRIBUTION: Scattered throughout sub-Saharan Africa in savanna grassland and bush, but eradicated from much of southern Africa by hunting and habitat loss.

SIZE: The world's largest land animal. Length up to 16.6ft (5m); height 7.8–13ft (2.4–4m); tail 39–59in (1–1.5m); weight 2.4–7 tons (2.2–6.3 tonnes). Males are taller and up to twice as heavy as females.

APPEARANCE: A huge, gray animal with a long trunk and pillarlike legs. The ears are larger than those of the Asian elephant, and the forehead is flat rather than domed. The back has a concave saddle just behind the shoulders. The trunk ends in two "fingers", while that of the Asian elephant ends in one. Both sexes have curved ivory tusks, which in males can grow over 11 feet (3.3m) long.

DIET: Mainly grass and leaves stripped from trees and shrubs, also roots, twigs, bark, and fruit.

Tusks are mainly used for digging up roots and stripping tree bark.

BREEDING: Elephants are long lived, with a life expectancy of up to 70 years. They breed slowly. Females usually mate for the first time at about 11 years old but even so, the earliest they can produce a calf is 13 because pregnancy lasts an amazing 22 months. Males are sexually mature at 10 years but few attain the size and strength required to see off rivals before they are 20 years old. Young are usually single, but twins do occur. The calf is dependent on its mother's milk for at least 18 months and remains in her care for several more years.

LIFESTYLE: African elephants are true gentle giants. Most live in close-knit family groups, centered on a single older female, the matriarch, who is usually mother, grandmother, sister, or aunt to all the others. All members of such a herd look out for the welfare of the others and appear to experience intense grief when one of them dies. Females remain in the same group all their lives, while males move away to join bachelor herds once they reach puberty. Males more than 25 years old undergo an annual period of "musth" during which elevated testosterone levels make them unusually aggressive and more likely to try to dominate other males. Musth bulls associate with female herds and will fight for the right to mate with estrus cows. African elephants have suffered cruelly at the hands of humans. They were hunted to the brink of extinction for their ivory and now depend on strict laws and international protection to survive.

PLAY FIGHT
Young African bull elephants tussle playfully. In later life, the sparring skills they learn may be brought to bear in earnest during the "musth" phase, when adult bulls fight for access to females.

INDIAN ELEPHANT

Elephas maximus
Family: ELEPHANTIDAE
Order: PROBOSCIDEA

DISTRIBUTION: Forests and grasslands of Asia and Indochina, from the Indian subcontinent and Sri Lanka to Malaysia, Indonesia and southern China. Habitat loss and the trade in ivory threaten the species with extinction.

SIZE: Length 18–22ft (5.5–6.6m); height 8-9.5ft (2.2.4–2.9m); weight 0.5–4.4 tons (0.5–4 tonnes). Males can grow twice as big as females.

APPEARANCE: A huge dark gray-brown animal with a long trunk, humped back, domed head and pillar-like legs. The ears are smaller than those of African elephants and the skin around the base of the trunk and chest is often mottled with pinkish blotches.

DIET: Mainly grasses, shoots, stems, leaves, vines and roots.

BREEDING: Females breed every 3–4 years between the ages of 10 and 55 years. Calves are born one, or occasionally two, at a time after a pregnancy lasting 21–22 months. The baby depends wholly on its mother's milk for 6 months, and will continue to suckle occasionally for up to 4 years. Longevity is up to 80 years.

LIFESTYLE: Indian elephants live in small family groups of females and young or in small bachelor herds. Mature males in "musth" (breeding condition) live alone and are aggressive towards other males. They wander more widely than usual in search of females. Once mating has taken place, males and females go their separate ways.
  Indian elephants eat and drink a lot – at least 330lb (150kg) of food and 11 gallons (50l) of water per day, and they are therefore dependent on well-vegetated habitats close to rivers or lakes. Their home ranges cover a wide area, anything from 15 to 115 square miles (40–300sq km) depending on the quality of habitat.

The species is threatened by habitat destruction caused by the logging industry. The elephants are forced to wander farther to find food and are often tempted to raid crops. Ivory poaching has a dramatic effect on sex ratios. Only the males are killed so that, in the Periyar Tiger Reserve in southern India for example, there is one male for every 100 females.

CAPTIVE SYMBOL
There are up to 15,000 Asian elephants living in captivity, many of which work in the timber trade. Elephants are also kept as status symbols in towns and cities, giving rise to concerns for their welfare.

AARDVARK

Orycteropus afer
Family: ORYCTEROPODIDAE
Order: TUBULIDENTATA

DISTRIBUTION: The aardvark is found in much of sub-Saharan Africa excluding the Congo Basin and Namib desert. Aardvarks favor grasslands, open woodland, and scrub, and are threatened by habitat loss and persecution.

SIZE: Length 3.3–5.3ft (1–1.6m); tail 17–24in (44–61cm); height 23–25in (60–65cm); width 110–181lb (50–82kg).

APPEARANCE: Also known as the ant bear and earth pig, this extraordinary pig-sized animal has a robust body, short limbs, and thick-based, tapering tail. However, the aardvark is best identified by its long cylindrical snout. The rabbit-like ears are long and tubular and can be folded back to avoid dirt when burrowing. The coat is coarse but thin and ranges from yellowish to brownish gray, often darker on the legs and paler on the head and tail – it may appear reddish when stained with soil.

DIET: Up to 50,000 ants and termites per night, lapped directly from nests and galleries in the earth. A feeding aardvark opens up an anthill or termite mound with its broad-clawed forefeet. It then sits down and pushes its snout into the hole, lapping up insects by the hundred with its long, sticky tongue.

BREEDING: A single young is born, just before the rainy season. Gestation is about 7 months, and the baby is suckled up to 6 months. Captive aardvarks have lived up to 23 years.

LIFESTYLE: One of Africa's most secretive animals, the aardvark lives alone and spends the daylight hours below ground in one of several burrows scattered about a large home range. The largest burrows may have several entrances as a security measure. At dusk the aardvark emerges, and spends the night following a vaguely circular foraging route and traveling up to 20 miles (30km) in 10 hours. An aardvark walks with its head down, and snout sweeping the ground to sniff out ant and termite nests. Its long, rabbitlike ears remain pricked and alert for sounds of potential predators.

Aardvarks are phenomenal diggers. Their broad, spoon-shaped front claws shovel even hard-packed earth so efficiently that the animal can bury itself in a matter of minutes. If threatened by a predator, such as a leopard, an aardvark can burrow very quickly and seek refuge below ground. It can also lash out at attackers with its claws.

FILTER SYSTEM
Hairs on the nostrils filter out dust and tiny insects excavated by the aardvark when it is digging.

PLAINS ZEBRA

Equus burchelli
Family: EQUIDAE
Order: PERISSODACTYLA

DISTRIBUTION: The world's most common wild horse is scattered in herds throughout southern and eastern Africa. Generally in savanna or lightly wooded areas away from forested and developed land and close to watering holes.

SIZE: Length 85–97in (2.17–2.46m); height 43–57in (1.10–1.45m); tail 18.5–22in (47–56cm); weight 385–350lb (175–385kg).

FEATURES: A stout, short-legged horse with a short erect mane and broad black stripes over the back, flanks, rump, head and neck but not always extending onto belly and legs. The black stripes sometimes alternate with pale brown lines.

DIET: Zebras eat mostly grass, but are not fussy and will graze tall, rank stems that other species avoid. They will also take other flowering plants and browse from trees.

BREEDING: Females breed every 1–2 years depending on conditions. Foals are born singly after a year-long gestation. Foals walk within 30 minutes and can run at one hour old. They first taste grass at about 1 week, but are not fully weaned for 7–11 months. Females are sexually mature at 16–22 months, males rarely breed before 4 years. Zebras may live up to 40 years in captivity, but much less in the wild.

LIFESTYLE: Plains zebras operate a harem system. Males acquire females by abducting fillies from existing herds. The excess males form bachelor groups of up to 15 individuals, within which bouts of play-fighting and chasing games are commonplace. Once breeding, mares will stay with a group for life. The whole harem helps protect young foals. Groups spend the night in special bedding areas, and commute to grazing pastures in the morning.

Plains zebras are non-territorial and the home ranges of several groups will overlap. Groups often come together to form huge herds, especially when food shortages cause seasonal migrations in search of good grazing. Zebras communicate using tactile and visual signals and a variety of horse- and donkey-like calls, though the sharp bark given by males is unique to the species.

SOCIAL STRIPES
Contrary to popular opinion, the zebra's stripes are probably not for camouflage. Zoologists now think that the unique pattern on each zebra acts as a social stimulus and help individuals recognize each other.

MALAYAN TAPIR

Tapirus indicus
Family: TAPIRIDAE
Order: PERISSODACTYLA

DISTRIBUTION: Southeast Asia, from Myanmar (Burma) and Thailand to peninsular Malaysia and Sumatra in rain forests and on the banks of rivers and lakes. Threatened by fragmentation of habitat and listed as vulnerable

SIZE: The largest of the world's tapir species; length 6–8ft (1.80–2.50m); height 3–3.6ft (0.9–1.1m); tail 2–4in (5–10cm); weight 330–700lb (150–320kg).

APPEARANCE: A robust, pig-like animal with a long fleshy snout, sturdy legs and very striking body markings. The back, rump, flanks and belly are white, the shoulders, head and legs are black. The pattern helps break up the animal's outline and is especially effective in dappled moonlight. Young tapirs are more subtly camouflaged, with dark brown fur marked with pale spots and stripes.

DIET: Grass, twigs and leaves of shrubs as well as aquatic plants.

Tapirs also use salt licks to supplement their mineral intake.

BREEDING: Young are born one at a time every other year in May-June after a 390–403 day gestation. The youngster receives its mother's undivided attention for 2 years, reaches sexual maturity at 3 years, and may live as long as 30 years.

LIFESTYLE: Like their South and Central American relatives, Malayan tapirs are efficient swimmers and spent a good deal of time in water, sometimes remaining submerged for several minutes at a time. On land they are surprisingly agile. They move fast through dense undergrowth and over steep ground, but the conspicuous trails they leave make them easy to track. Malayan tapirs are preyed upon by tigers and leopards. When pursued they make directly for the water, which in itself does not deter the big cats, but it makes the tapir's scent much less easy to follow. Cool water and mud are also a good way for the tapirs to rid themselves of flies.

Apart from mothers with young, Malayan tapirs are solitary. They live alone in overlapping home ranges, using scent and shrill whistling calls to keep other tapirs informed of their whereabouts in the dark forest. Tapirs also like to wallow in mud. They are excellent swimmers and spend much time in water feeding and cooling off. If alarmed they can remain submerged for several minutes. Man is the tapir's most dangerous predator – tapirs are prized for their flesh, and their meat is often sold illegally for a high price. There is also a continued trade in live animals for private collectors.

TRUNK-LIKE

The tapir's nose and upper lip combine to form a flexible, muscular snout called the proboscis. Like a smaller version of an elephant's trunk, the proboscis is used for smelling and selectively plucking the best food.

WHITE RHINO

Ceratotherium simum
Family: RHINOCEROTIDAE
Order: PERISSODACTYLA

DISTRIBUTION: Scattered remnants of formerly widespread population exist in southern Africa and the Democratic Republic of Congo. The species is restricted to protected areas with flat, lightly forested grassy plains close to water.

SIZE: Length 11–14ft (3.35–4.20m); height 5–6ft (1.50–1.85m); tail 20–27.5in (50–70cm); weight 1.5–2.7 tons (1.4–2.5 tonnes). Males are 20–90 percent bigger than females.

APPEARANCE: A huge animal with a barrel-shaped body, short, sturdy legs, a large head and a distinctive hump between the shoulders. There are two horns, one on the tip of the snout and one further back. Its short, thick legs and wide feet help to spread its great weight.

DIET: This is the largest pure grass eater alive today. The white rhino's square lips and high-crowned cheek teeth are specially adapted for processing tough grasses. It is also dependent upon water, drinking almost daily at small pools, or rivers. They can survive 4–5 days between waterhole visits.

BREEDING: Calves are born singly at any time of year after a 16 month gestation. Newborns can stand almost immediately and have no horns. They wean at 12–14 months and reach sexually maturity at 5 years, though males may not breed until they are 10–12 years old. Rhinos live up to 50 years.

LIFESTYLE: White rhinos are active by day and night, but feed mostly in the morning and evening. They love to wallow in mud, which helps to cool them and to get rid of skin parasites. When not wallowing, they rest in shady areas during the heat of the day.

Adult females use home ranges of up to 4 square miles (10sq km) and usually have at least one youngster tagging along. Mature males live alone on territories as small as 2 acres (0.75sq km). They mark out their territories with dung heaps, urine, and foot scrapes. Both sexes are surprisingly vocal, and use a range of grunts, squeaks, squeals, growls, bellows and panting sounds. White rhinos are a variable shade of grayish brown. The white in their name is a corruption of the African word *widje*, meaning wide, referring to its wide mouth.

SQUARE LIP
The characteristic square lip gives the white rhino a wide area of bite, which compensates for the shortness of the grasses it prefers to eat.

WARTHOG

Phacochoerus africanus
Family: SUIDAE
Order: ARTIODACTYLA

DISTRIBUTION: African savanna from Mauritania to Ethiopia and south to Namibia and South Africa.

SIZE: Length 4.6–4.4ft (1.1–1.35m); height 22–34in (55–85cm); tail 16in (40cm); weight 110–220lb (50–100kg).

APPEARANCE: A relatively slim, long-legged pig with pronounced facial warts. Both males and females have prominent curved tusks in the upper jaw and smaller, sharper ones in the lower jaw. The skin is gray with sparse black hairs and a beard of paler bristles.

DIET: Mostly plant matter including grass, roots, berries, and bark. Warthogs are opportunists and will also take advantage of animal remains too.

BREEDING: Courtship happens late in the rainy season and young are born early the next rainy season after a 170–175 days gestation period. Litters can contain up to 8 piglets, but most females raise just 2 or 3 at a time, caring for them in a burrow. They are weaned by 6 months, sexually mature at about 18 months and may live up to 18 years.

LIFESTYLE: Warthogs are unusual among pigs in that they are active mostly during the day and are better adapted for grazing than for rooting around for food below the surface, although they still do this where the ground is not too hard. The typical grazing posture is kneeling, with the front legs folded beneath the chest.

Warthogs are highly social. They live in large inter-related groups called clans, within which females live in groups called "sounders," comprising closely related individuals (such as sisters, mothers, daughters). Juvenile boars may form temporary bachelor groups but become solitary as adults.

Clans are generally peaceful. Individuals share burrows and resources amicably, engage in social activities such as mutual grooming and appear to show a great deal of affection towards one another. In the breeding season adult males compete for access to groups of females. Fighting is not uncommon, but is highly ritualized so serious injuries are comparatively rare.

HIGH TAILING IT

Warthogs are alert to their surroundings and although their eyesight is poor they have very acute hearing. Individuals respond quickly to disturbance, moving away at a brisk trot or fast gallop with the tail held high. They need to move swiftly as they are preyed upon by big cats, including cheetahs.

HIPPOPOTAMUS

Hippopotamus amphibius
Family: HIPPOPOTAMIDAE
Order: ARTIODACTYLA

DISTRIBUTION: West, Central, East and South Africa, in rivers and nearby grasslands.

SIZE: Length 10.8–11.3ft (3.3–3.45m); height 4.6ft (1.4m); tail 14–18in (35-50cm); weight 1.5 to as much as 3.5 tons (1.4–3.2 tonnes) in extreme cases.

APPEARANCE: A huge, vaguely pig-like animal with a large head, a broad expanded muzzle and a thin tail. The mouth is enormous and opens to 150 degrees to display long, razor sharp tusks. The eyes and ears are small and positioned high on the head. The hippo's skin is naked and greasy looking. The pigment of the upper body is dark gray to brown, while the under parts are pinkish. There are 4 toes on each foot.

DIET: Mainly grasses, grazed from the savanna at night.

BREEDING: Female hippos breed from the age of 9 years. Mating occurs mainly in the dry season. Calves are born singly, usually in the water after a gestation of about 240 days. The youngster is weaned at 6–8 months and can expect to live about 45 years.

LIFESTYLE: The traditional picture of hippopotamuses is of a large herd wallowing in a river or pool. In fact this is where hippos go to rest during the day. The water supports their great bulk and thus saves them a lot of energy. It helps keep them cool and protects their naked skin from the sun. It also prevents dehydration, since hippo skin loses water very easily when exposed to dry air. However, hippos do not feed in the water. At night they lumber ashore and travel independently inland to graze on rich grasslands, then return to the same water before dawn.

Another commonly held view is that hippos are dangerously aggressive. This is not a misconception! All hippos seem bad tempered at the best of times. The animals crammed together in a watering hole are forced to spend the day living cheek by jowl, but there is continual jostling for space, accompanied by rumbling growls and grunts. Dominant males defend a long stretch of river or lake shore and claim exclusive breeding rights to the females there. Small, submissive males may be allowed to live within the territory unmolested, but challenges to the lead male's dominance will not be tolerated.

While many territorial disputes are settled with displays such as glaring and spattering feces, fights between rival males still break out frequently.

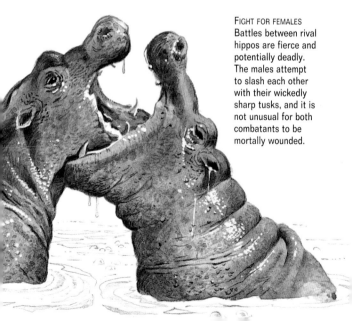

FIGHT FOR FEMALES
Battles between rival hippos are fierce and potentially deadly. The males attempt to slash each other with their wickedly sharp tusks, and it is not unusual for both combatants to be mortally wounded.

BACTRIAN CAMEL

Camelus bactrianus
Family: CAMELIDAE
Order: ARTIODACTYLA

DISTRIBUTION: Wild Bactrian camels are critically endangered and live only on the steppes and rocky deserts of north-western China and Mongolia. There is a domesticated population of some 2 million.

SIZE: Length 7.4–11.3ft (2.25–3.45m); height 6–7.25ft (1.9–2.3m); tail 14–21in (35–55cm); weight 660–1500lb (300–690kg).

APPEARANCE: A tall, rangy animal with long legs, a long neck and 2 prominent humps on its back. The head looks disproportionately small and has round ears, large eyes and a split, fleshy upper lip. The feet are broad with two hoofed toes and soft pads and there are callused "sitting patches" on the knees and chest.

DIET: Mostly plant material, but can make a meal of almost anything, including animal remains, even bones and leather.

BREEDING: Females give birth to one calf every other year in spring after a 12–14 month gestation. The young are able to run within an hour of birth, but remain in their mother's care for up to 2 years. They are weaned at 12–18 months and sexual maturity comes at about 3 years. Camels can live up to 50 years.

LIFESTYLE: The Bactrian camel is superbly adapted to life in arid deserts where temperatures range from 40°C (104°F) by day in summer to winter nighttime lows of -29°C (-20°F). The shaggy wool on the camel's back and neck keep it warm when it lies down at night and the thinner coat of its belly allows breezes to cool it during the day. The animal can survive fluctuations in body temperature that would kill most other mammals. The Bactrian has closeable nostrils to keep out dust, and can survive by drinking salty water if need be. Wild camels live alone or in non-territorial groups of up to 30 individuals. They need a lot of space because food is scarce. Groups move around their home range in single file, feeding sparingly over a wide area. Mature males guard harems and will fight each other for possession of females.

FAT STORE
The twin humps of the Bactrian camel are used to store fat. If the camel is badly nourished they become thin and floppy.

LLAMA

Lama glama
Family: CAMELIDAE
Order: ARTIODACTYLA

DISTRIBUTION: Most llamas live under domestication in the Andes region of South America. Feral animals occupy grassland and scrub at high altitudes up to 13,000ft (4,000m).

SIZE: Length 47–88in (120–225cm); height 42–45in (109–119cm); weight 285–340lb (130–155kg).

APPEARANCE: A leggy, longnecked animal with a short tail and a thick fleece of beige to dark brown wool. The head is small, with a split upper lip and the eyes and ears are large. There are 2 hoofed toes on each foot.

DIET: Mainly grasses and leaves, including trees and shrubs.

BREEDING: Female llamas are induced ovulators – the act of mating stimulates their ovaries to release an egg, which is fertilized immediately. Gestation takes 11–11.5 months and the young (called "crias") are born from

November to February. They are able to run at less than 1 hour old. They are weaned at 6–8 months, sexually mature at 1 year and may live well over 20 years.

LIFESTYLE: Llamas are adapted to life at high altitude. Their blood has an unusually high capacity for oxygen, allowing them to make the most of very thin mountain air. The soft underfur of the fleece provides insulation against the cold, while the coarse guard hairs that overlie them protect against rain and snow. Llamas keep their wool in good condition by rolling in dust to remove excess grease and parasites. Their long legs enable them to travel great distances in search of grazing, while their long necks allow them to graze while standing.

Llamas are social animals and family groups comprise females and young, dominated by a single territorial adult male. Juveniles are

driven away as they approach maturity. The females join another harem where they can breed, while young males spend three or four years in bachelor herds until they are strong enough to defend a harem of their own. All adult llamas have a guarding instinct and will tackle predators to defend the herd and seem unwilling to abandon sick or injured members of the group.

PACK ANIMALS
Llamas are a domesticated species. Most work as pack animals or are kept as livestock, supplying wool and meat.

REINDEER

Rangifer tarandus
Family: CERVIDAE
Order: ARTIDACTYLA

DISTRIBUTION: Taiga, woodland margins and tundra throughout the Arctic Circle including Alaska, Canada, Greenland, Scandinavia and Russia. Some populations undertake seasonal migrations of up to 3,000 miles (5,000km).

SIZE: Length 6.1–7.3ft (1.85–2.2m); height male 3.5–4.2ft (1.1–1.3m); tail 4–6in (10–15cm); weight 200–600lb (90–270kg). Males are generally 10–20 percent larger than females, and "caribou", as they are called in North America, tend to be larger than the Eurasian reindeer.

APPEARANCE: A large deer, dark brown in summer, but grayish in the winter due to long pale hairs in winter coat. There are white patches on the rump, tail and on each foot. The head is large, with proportionately small ears – an adaptation to reduce heat loss. The feet are broad, with cloven hooves that splay out as the reindeer walks, spreading its weight and thereby allowing it to walk on mud, moss and snow without sinking. Both sexes sport large, irregularly branched antlers up to 50 inches (130cm) long

DIET: Lichens, especially "reindeer moss" (*Cladonia rangiferina*), sedges and grass, also browses leaves from trees and shrubs.

BREEDING: Reindeer rut in early fall. A single calf, rarely twins, is born after gestation of 210–240 days and weaned at one month. Females survive up to 15 years in the wild, males are less long-lived.

LIFESTYLE: Reindeer are gregarious animals. In spring they sometimes gather in huge numbers, moving northward *en masse* in order to exploit the short but productive Arctic summer. Over the summer the majority live in small herds led by experienced females. The extended daylight means that the

ANTLERED FEMALES

Reindeer are unusual among deer in that both sexes bear antlers. It is possible that females find antlers beneficial in defending winter feeding areas, which they have had to work hard to clear of packed snow. Males will clash their antlers in ritualized sparring, and this merely serves as a test of strength rather than leading to bloodshed.

herds can feed almost nonstop, pausing to rest every few hours. Calves are born in midsummer and soon afterwards the female herds become the subject of disputes between rutting males.

RED DEER

Cervus elaphus
Family: CERVIDAE
Order: ARTIODACTYLA

DISTRIBUTION: Temperate Europe and Central Asia, from the British Isles to Tibet, with scattered populations in Scandinavia and around the Mediterranean. Most populations favor woodland habitats but some also live on open hillsides and in deer parks.

SIZE: Length 5.4–8.5ft (1.65–2.6m); height about 4ft (1.2m); tail 6–8in (15–20cm); weight 165–750lb (75–340kg). Red deer size varies with geographic range but males are always bigger than females.

APPEARANCE: This large deer is named for its short summer coat, which grows a rich shade of reddish brown. The winter coat is dark brown and shaggy. There is a creamy-orange rump patch all year round. Only males grow antlers.

DIET: Red deer browse leaves and shoots from a variety of trees and shrubs. In winter they turn their attention to grass and sedges.

BREEDING: The breeding season, or rut, happens in the fall. Calves are born the following spring after a gestation lasting 235–265 days. Most are single offspring, though twins do occur. Females live up to 25 years; males live for far less.

LIFESTYLE: Red deer living in different parts of the northern hemisphere have adopted different lifestyles in order to best exploit the available resources. The species does best in forested areas. Here there is plentiful food, the deer are sheltered from severe weather and stand a better chance of evading predators. Red deer are highly gregarious. For most of the year they live in single sex groups but during the breeding season, or rut, they assemble in the same breeding area each year. Males attempt to prove their superiority through ritualized displays and by fighting, and females choose to mate with the strongest males.

DISPOSABLE ASSETS
Males grow branching antlers every year – the number of "tines" (points) is an indicator of age and nutritional health.

MOOSE

Alces alces
Family: CERVIDAE
Order: ARTIODACTYLA

DISTRIBUTION: Northern Europe, Siberia, Mongolia, Manchuria, Alaska, Canada and northeastern coterminous United States, in woodland and adjacent open country.

SIZE: The world's largest deer species. Length: 5.25–9.5ft (1.6–2.9m); height 5.6–7.5ft (1.5–2.3m); tail 3–4in (7–10cm); weight 600–1760lb (275–800kg). Males are taller and heftier than females.

APPEARANCE: The moose has a large head and body and long, slender legs. Its coats is brown, paler on the belly. A ball of flesh called the "bell" hangs loosely from the throat. Males regrow large, palmate antlers spanning up to 5 feet (1.5m), with 18–20 "tines" (points).

DIET: Herbs, leaves and aquatic plants when available, but the species eats huge quantities of tree shoots and twigs in winter.

The name moose comes from a Native American word meaning "twig-eater."

BREEDING: Mating takes place in September and October. Gestation lasts 240–250 days and calves are born singly or as twins, occasionally triplets in May and June. The calves are precocious and are weaned at 5 months. Females usually live longer than males – up to 20 years.

LIFESTYLE: Moose dislike warm weather. In summer they restrict their movements to shady places with easy access to pools and lakes, where they can bathe and feed at the same time. Moose are excellent swimmers, and spend a lot of time in water. They can dive for up to a minute and often head for water when trying to escape a predator. During spring and summer moose live more or less alone. They gather into herds in the fall and the rut begins in late September. Bull mooses wallow in mud and spray urine onto their own fur, and rivals engage in ritualized displays, charges and shoving matches. The encounter may escalate to a fight with antlers.

SMALL REALTY
Moose use home ranges of less than 4 square miles (10sq km) in area – quite small for such large animals.

RETICULATED GIRAFFE

Giraffa camelopardalis
Family: GIRAFFIDAE
Order: ARTIODACTYLA

DISTRIBUTION: The giraffe is only found in the wild in savanna areas of Africa south of the Sahara.

SIZE: Total height (head to feet) up to 16ft (5.2m); weight: 1,800–1930lb (450–1,180kg). Females are smaller and less heavily built than bulls.

APPEARANCE: The giraffe's immensely long neck and legs make it the tallest living mammal. The back slopes down from the shoulders to the hips. There is a thin, brush-ended tail. The coat of the reticulated giraffe is distinctive, with regular blocks of red brown hair broken by a network of fine white lines. The head is small and tapering and males have 4 hairy "horns" on the forehead.

DIET: Giraffes feed selectively, plucking the best leaves from a wide variety of savanna trees and shrubs using their long neck and 18 inch (45cm) long tongue to reach high into the branches.

BREEDING: Giraffes mature at 3–4 years, but breed slowly. Females rear a single calf (rarely twins) at 2–3 year intervals – gestation alone takes 450–465 days. Longevity is normally about 20 years.

LIFESTYLE: Reticulated giraffes (*Giraffa camelopardalis reticulata*) live in rather casual groups, comprising animals that may or may not be related. Males wander more widely than females and will fight for temporary control of a group containing a female that is ready to mate. However the association is short-lived and the members of a group change from day to day.

Giraffes appear to run in slow motion due to their very long legs and unusual rocking gait, but their long legs can carry them to a maximum speed of 35mph (56kmh) and they have considerable stamina. Even fast-running predators, though speedier, give up after a short chase. Giraffes are more vulnerable on soft ground, for example around drinking holes. During dry weather they are forced to remain in such areas, not just to drink, but to feed on trees than remain green while those on the open plain become dry. In the rainy season they disperse more widely. Giraffes are known to neck wrestle – it's a sort of ritualized fighting indulged by many young bulls to determine dominance. The necks are slowly intertwined pushing from one side to the other.

If a bout fails to establish a clear winner the rival giraffes may resort to a more drastic form of battle, delivering potentially lethal kicks with their back legs.

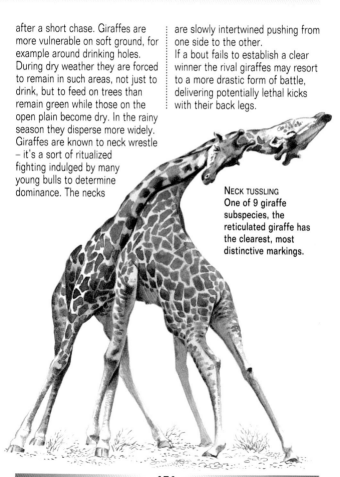

NECK TUSSLING
One of 9 giraffe subspecies, the reticulated giraffe has the clearest, most distinctive markings.

PRONGHORN

Antilocapra americana
Family: ANTILOCAPRIDAE
Order: ARTIODACTYLA

DISTRIBUTION: This species has responded well to conservation measures and populations totalling 1 million now occupy rolling grassland and dry bush habitats of the western USA, Canada, and parts of northern Mexico.

SIZE: Length 3.8–4.4ft (1.16–1.33m); height 34in (87cm); tail 4–5.5in (10–14cm); weight 90–130lb (42–59kg). Males are a little bigger than females.

APPEARANCE: Resembling stocky antelope with unusual horns in the male – these have a backward-curving tip and stout forward-pointing prong. Female pronghorns also have horns but these tend to be very small and unbranched. The coat is pale brown, fading to white on the flanks, throat, belly, and rump. Males have a black face mask and patches beneath the ears.

DIET: Grasses, herbs, and shrubs, occasionally crops and cacti.

BREEDING: Females give birth to twins in spring after a gestation period of around 8.5 months. The fawns can run fast within days. They are fully weaned at 4–5 months. Females usually start breeding at 16 months, males take longer to gain the size, strength, and social dominance to compete effectively for mates. Wild pronghorns live about 10 years.

LIFESTYLE: Pronghorns are active and alert. Their long legs help make them the fastest quadrupeds in North America, capable of speeds over 55mph (86kmh). This spectacular turn of speed developed as an adaptation to escape predators, though today these are relatively few.

Pronghorns live in small bands year round and in the fall, these form herds several hundred strong. Males engage in ritualized displays, staring matches, chases, and ultimately fighting by locking horns and shoving each other in order to

acquire and defend territories. Females select mates based on the quality of habitat in their territory. By competing for good habitat, males are effectively vying for females. In spring, the large aggregations break up into smaller herds once more, some all male, others comprising females and their newborn young. Yearlings may also remain with their mothers, and females usually stay within their mother's herd for life.

SOLE SURVIVOR
The pronghorn is the only animal of its kind – the last survivor of a once successful group of American ungulates.

153

WATER BUFFALO

Bubalus bubalis (B. arnee)
Family: BOVIDAE
Order: ARTIODACTYLA

DISTRIBUTION: Wild water buffalo once lived from Nepal and India as far east as Vietnam and the Malay Peninsula and on the islands of Sri Lanka, Sumatra, Java, and Borneo. They have been replaced in many parts by domesticated versions of the same species. Pure-bred wild specimens are now extremely difficult to find. They favor swamps and wetlands.

SIZE: Length 6.5–10ft (2–3m); height 58–74in (1.5–1.9m); tail 23–39in (0.6–1m); weight 0.9–1.3 tons (800–1,200kg). The horns can span as much as 6.5ft (2m).

APPEARANCE: A large gray or black ox with short legs and very large curved horns. The face is long and the ears are large and slightly droopy with fringed edges. The feet have two splaying toes with large hooves, to help the animal walk over soft mud.

DIET: Grasses, ferns, and shoots, fruits, and leaves of small trees.

BREEDING: Females breed every other year, giving birth to just one calf after a gestation of 300–340 days. The calf is suckled for up to 9 months and reaches puberty at about 18 months. Wild water buffalo live to 25 years (30 in captivity).

LIFESTYLE: Herds of water buffalo are kept as livestock throughout much of the species' natural range. In the wild females and young also live as herds, led by an older female. The herds usually number less than 20, but may join up with others at the end of the day in bedding areas. Most males live in bachelor groups but older bulls are often solitary.
   Male and female herds remain separate throughout the dry season and males wander widely. At the start of the wet season in October the sexes mix and males compete for access to females in estrus. Females with calves from the previous year are aggressive and intolerant of males.

WATER LOVERS
Water buffalo drink
a lot of water and
appear to relish
wallowing in mud.
This helps keep them
cool and rids their
skin of irritating flies
and parasites.

AFRICAN BUFFALO

Syncerus caffer
Family: BOVIDAE
Order: ARTIODACTYLA

DISTRIBUTION: Buffalo range widely over western, central and eastern Africa, south of the Sahara Desert. They mostly favor savanna woodland close to water but there is also a smaller forest-dwelling form.

SIZE: Length 7.9–11.25ft (2.40–3.4m); height 4.5–5.6ft (1.35–1.70m); tail 30–44in (0.75–1.1m); weight 550–1,870lb (250–850kg). Males are especially massive.

APPEARANCE: A large ox with sparse black to reddish-brown hair and huge curved horns that meet on top of the head. The ears are large and droop beneath the horns.

DIET: Mainly grass, but a wide variety of swamp vegetation is also eaten.

BREEDING: Breeding is seasonal, but varies from place to place depending on the timing of the annual rains. A single large calf is born after a gestation of around 340 days. It stays close to its mother for 2 years or more after which females remain in their mother's herd, but young males usually disperse. Sexual maturity reached at 3–5 years and average longevity in the wild is about 18 years.

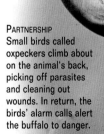

PARTNERSHIP
Small birds called oxpeckers climb about on the animal's back, picking off parasites and cleaning out wounds. In return, the birds' alarm calls alert the buffalo to danger.

LIFESTYLE: African buffalo are social and gregarious. They sometimes gather in herds of up to several hundred individuals in wet places with plenty of food and wallowing holes. Individuals tend to remain in the same herd for life and rarely wander far. Herd home ranges are often as little as 4 square miles (10sq km).

Buffalo herds are usually made up of a dozen animals and consist of social groups comprising females with their young of several years. There are also groups of bachelor males, within which there is a rank order based on size and strength. Males will sometimes fight to determine rank, but for the most part these are peaceful animals.

African buffalo remain wary at all times and their big, droopy ears give them very sensitive hearing.

AMERICAN BISON

Bison bison
Family: BOVIDAE
Order: ARTIODACTYLA

DISTRIBUTION: The former prairie population of about 50 million was reduced to just 541 in 1887 as a result of merciless hunting. Intensive conservation has repaired some of the damage and today there are large herds throughout the Midwestern USA, especially in Wyoming and South Dakota. The total population is upwards of 200,000.

SIZE: Length 6.9–12.5ft (2.1–3.8m); height up to 6.5ft (1.9m); tail 17–36 in (43–90cm); weight 790–2,000lb (360–907kg).

APPEARANCE: A huge, ox-like animal, with a massive head and shoulders. The forelegs neck, chest and shoulders are covered in shaggy dark brown hair. Both sexes carry curved horns.

DIET: Mostly grazers of grass and various sedges and herbs. They also sometimes browse shrubs such as willow, sagebrush and birch.

BREEDING: Calves arrive in early summer after a gestation period of 9–10 months. They can run within 3 hours and begin eating grass at 1 week. They are fully weaned at about 6 months and capable of breeding at 2–3 years old. Lifespan up to 25 years in the wild.

BIGGEST AMERICAN MAMMAL
The bison is the biggest animal in the Americas. Males are bigger and up to three times heavier than females. Smaller specimens known as wood bison live in south western Canada.

LIFESTYLE: Bison are active day and night. They move slowly, grazing as they go. Where they still have freedom to roam, they undertake some seasonal movements, using higher pastures in summer. They spend much of their time resting, and seem to enjoy bathing in dust or mud. They are alert, wary, and easily spooked. They can run at nearly 40mph (60kmh). Bison herds normally comprise a few dozen animals. Mature males live alone or in small groups and join up with the females in summer for the rut.

BRINDLED GNU

Connochaetes taurinus
Family: BOVIDAE
Order: ARTIODACTYLA

DISTRIBUTION: African savanna woodland and grassy plains south from Kenya to north-western Mozambique and from Zambia to South Africa. Some populations undertake lengthy migrations at beginning and end of the dry season.

SIZE: Length 68–96in (1.7–2.4m); tail 24–39in (0.6–1m); height 46–58in (1.15–1.45m); weight 308–638lb (140–290kg). Males are a little larger than females.

APPEARANCE: The gnu's somewhat ungainly appearance compared with other antelope belies its speed and agility. Its large head, humped shoulders and deep neck give it an ox-like appearance, while its legs and hindquarters are slim and appear out of proportion. Large horns curl upward and inward at the tip. The coat is dark gray tinged with brown and there is a mane of longer darker hair clearly visible around the neck, chin and shoulders.

DIET: Grass.

BREEDING: Births within a herd are highly synchronized, with almost all females producing single calves within a 2-week period after a pregnancy lasting 243–274 days. Females are sexually mature at about 16 months; males begin to breed at about 4 or 5 years. Lifespan is up to 20 years.

LIFESTYLE: Gnus are gregarious. Their social organization comprises solitary territorial older males, bachelor groups of younger males and female herds, all of which congregate in areas where there is plentiful short grass and water. Newly independent males will leave the herd they were born in and join a bachelor group, but females tend to stay in their mother's herd. The herding instinct is a vital survival strategy since gnus form the staple of many carnivores' diet. Stragglers fall prey to lions, cheetahs, leopards, spotted hyenas, and crocodiles. Activity within the herds peaks in early morning and late afternoon, and they rest during the hottest part of day. They often graze alongside other herbivores such

as zebra. Some populations, like those of the Great Rift Valley make annual mass migrations in search of grazing and water.

FOOD CHAIN
Gnus make up 60 percent of the large mammal population of the Serengeti and Masai Mara game reserves. They play a major part in savanna ecology, consuming vast quantities of grass and in their turn providing food, especially for lions and hyenas.

SPRINGBOK

Antidorcas marsupialis
Family: BOVIDAE
Order: ARTIODACTYLA

DISTRIBUTION: Plains, savanna and other dry habitats in Southern Angola, Namibia, Botswana and South Africa.

SIZE: Length: 4–5ft (1.2–1.5m); tail 5.5–11in (14–28cm); height 27–36in (68–90cm); weight 44–130lb (20–60kg). Males are larger than females.

APPEARANCE: This graceful antelope has cinnamon-brown upper parts, a dark brown band on each flank and white under parts. The rump and tail are white and there is a crest of white hair along the lower back. The head is small and elegant with long, leaf-shaped ears and short, ridged horns in both sexes.

DIET: Favor fresh, sweet grass when available and switch to leaves and flowers of shrubs in the dry season. They also dig up roots and tubers. Plant juices provide sufficient moisture that they rarely need to drink water.

BREEDING: Females begin breeding at the tender age of at 7 months and may rear one young a year for 8 or 9 years. Males mature slower and will not breed until they can defend a territory. Gestation lasts 6 months and longevity is 10 years or more.

LIFESTYLE: The springbok is renowned for its athleticism – hence its adoption as the symbol of the South African international rugby team. The most characteristic display of physical prowess is "stotting", when the animal repeatedly springs stiff-legged into the air. Springboks do this when they are alarmed or being chased, and sometimes it seems, just for fun. Herds are smaller than they once were, and great migrations, during which hundreds of thousands traveled together in search of fresh grass are a thing of the past. Today, farming restricts their movements.

THE HEAT IS ON
Springboks are active in daytime, but take a siesta around midday. They avoid overheating by resting in the shade and turning their white rumps to the sun to reflect he worst of the heat.

THOMSON'S GAZELLE

Gazella thomsoni
Family: BOVIDAE
Order: ARTIODACTYLA

DISTRIBUTION: Savanna grasslands in Tanzania, Kenya, and southern Sudan.

SIZE: Length 2.7–4ft (0.8–1.2m); tail 6–11in (15–27cm); height 22–33in (55–82cm); weight 33–77lb (15–35kg). Males are larger than females.

APPEARANCE: This small, dainty antelope has a light brown coat, a white rump and underside and a bold black band along each flank. The tail is also black and the face is marked with white eye rings and a black stripe on each cheek. Both sexes have ridged s-shaped horns, those of males are longer and thicker than females.

DIET: Mostly fresh green grass in the rainy season, switching to herbs, foliage and seeds in the dry.

BREEDING: Adult males compete for territories, scent marking liberally and locking horns in fights to determine dominance. Males without territories have very limited opportunities to mate, so the stakes are high. In good habitat females can breed twice annually from the age of 9 months, producing 1 or 2 young at a time after a gestation period of 5–6 months. Lifespan is approximately 10 years.

LIFESTYLE: Thomson's gazelles are highly social and live in large herds. The day-to-day movements of the herd are dictated by an experienced female, but each group is defended by a single mature male. Herds sometimes throng together to migrate in search of better food. They often graze alongside gnus and zebra, taking advantage of the larger species' habit of grazing down tall grasses, which gives the gazelles access to tender new shoots growing close to the ground.

Thomson's gazelles are animals of the open plain. In the absence of any cover in which to hide, they rely on speed, agility and safety in numbers to protect them from predators including lions, cheetahs, hyenas and jackals. All members of a herd are vigilant and if one spots a predator it will alert its companions. The gazelles then adopt the unexpected strategy of advancing on the predator, thus drawing attention to it and ruining its chances of a surprise attack. They remain poised to flee should the predator call their bluff, and the confusion created by dozens of gazelles bounding in all direction is often enough to foil the attack.

A SERIOUS GAME
Thomson's gazelles are exceptionally agile. Young animals delight in practicing huge bounds and mid-air changes of direction – their games prepare them well for survival.

MUSK OX

Ovibos moschatus
Family: BOVIDAE
Order: ARTIODACTYLA

DISTRIBUTION: Arctic tundra in Greenland and northern Canada, introduced populations live in Alaska and central Scandinavia. Populations are recovering from being hunted in the 19th century.

SIZE: Length 6.3–8.7ft (1.9.–2.65m); height 4–5ft (1.2–1.5m); tail 2.5–4.75in (7–12cm); weight: 350–900lb (160–410kg).

APPEARANCE: A stocky animal with humped shoulders, short legs, and a thick, shaggy black coat that reaches almost to the ground in winter. The underwool is thick but very fine and covers all extremities including the ears, tail, scrotum, and udder. Both sexes have sharp, curved horns, those of females are smaller and lack a central boss.

DIET: Grasses, lichens, sedges, herbs, and stunted tundra shrubs.

BREEDING: The mating season is August and September and young are born, usually singly, 8–9 months later in spring. Females breed in alternate years from the age of 2, males reach maturity at 5. Longevity is at least 24 years.

LIFESTYLE: Herds of up to 50 musk oxen gather in winter and members benefit from shared body heat in bad weather and cooperate to protect their young. When threatened, they form a tight circle with youngsters in the center and the adults facing outward to confront the threat with a wall of heavy bodies and bristling horns.

In summer females and young form smaller herds and males become solitary or live in groups of 2–5. In August and September, dominant males acquire harems of females and deter rivals with bellowing, displays of strength, and scent marking. When two males fight, they charge at one other and clash heads until one of them backs down.

SLOW MOVER
The musk ox moves
slowly, traveling as little
as possible to conserve
energy. It spends most
of its waking hours
looking for food.

MOUNTAIN GOAT

Oreamnos americanus
Family: BOVIDAE
Order: ARTIODACTYLA

DISTRIBUTION: The mountain goat lives on crags and steep rocky terrain. Its range extends from southeastern Alaska, through south Yukon and south-west Mackenzie to Oregon, Idaho, and Montana. There are introduced populations elsewhere in North America.

SIZE: Length 45–63in (1.15–1.6m); tail 3–8in (8–20cm); height 33–48in (0.8–1.22m); weight 101–309lb (46–140kg). Males are bigger and heavier than females.

APPEARANCE: The mountain goat's thick woolly coat makes it look thickset and stocky. The white fleece serves as camouflage in snow and keeps the animal warm. The outer coat of long hairs allows water to sluice off so the underfleece stays dry. Males and females have black, curving horns 6–8 inches (15–25cm) long, but thicker in males. The feet are adapted for climbing, with hard, sharp hooves around flexible rubbery pads providing sure grip.

DIET: Goats eat pretty much any plants that are available including a wide range of trees, shrubs, grasses, and herbs

BREEDING: Mating happens during November and December and single young or twins are born in May and June after a gestation of about 180 days. The kids are weaned at 3 months. Longevity is between 12 and 16 years – males tend to die younger than females because of the additional stress of the rut.

LIFESTYLE: For most of the year adult mountain goats avoid one another's company. If forced together by limited food resources females with young tend to dominate other adults in order to gain the best food for their kid. Males become increasingly aggressive and agitated in the rutting season. They mark grass and tree branches with scent from

glands at the base of their horns
and roll in latrines to cover
themselves in a smelly mixture of
dirt and urine. They engage in
head-tossing displays and fight by
jostling flank to flank and trying to
stab each other's rump and flanks
with their horns.

HIGH LIFE
Mountain goats spend
most of their lives on
high rocky ledges, where
they can browse or rest
safely out of reach of
predators such as
coyotes and lynx. In
severe weather, the
goats may be forced
onto lower pastures.

AMERICAN BIGHORN SHEEP

Ovis canadensis
Family: BOVIDAE
Order: ARTIODACTYLA

DISTRIBUTION: Southwestern Canada through the western USA to northern Mexico, in rocky terrain with partial cover from dry deserts to high alpine territory. The population is considered secure but requires conservation to keep it that way.

SIZE: Length 4.75–6.1ft (1.45–1.86m); tail 2.7–4.7in (7–12cm); weight 125–310lb (57–140kg). Males can weigh three times as much as females.

APPEARANCE: A stocky brown sheep with a white face and predominantly brown fleece, the under parts and rump are paler. Ewes have short straight horns, those of males spiral backward from the head and can grow very large indeed.

DIET: Mainly tough grasses, also herbs and some shrubs.

BREEDING: Mating occurs during fall and early winter. Pregnant females gestate one young at a time and give birth after 175 days. The lamb is weaned around 4–5 months. Females are sexually mature at 4–5 years, males first breed at 6–7 years, when they are big enough to compete for mates. Longevity is greater in females, which might live 20 years.

LIFESTYLE: Bighorn sheep are exceptionally hardy and amazingly agile. They can leap up steep, rocky slopes at speed and negotiate the narrowest of rock ledges with confident ease. Bighorns are sociable animals, and spend most of the year in small non-territorial groups comprising bachelor males and females with young. Bands wander casually within a home range of anything up to 8 square miles (20sq km). There is an overall shift to lower altitudes in winter. The bands sometimes congregate into large herds. Bighorns are active by day, but still rest frequently. At night, they retreat to sleep, often on secure ledges, sometimes even in caves where predators such as wolves and mountain lions cannot approach unseen. Bighorns have excellent eyesight. During the rut males become aggressive, and dominant individuals display their magnificent horns to deter rivals. Sometimes the display escalates to violence, with rivals head butting and attempting to shunt each other off ledges.

HORN OF PLENTY
Females have small, straight horns while the massive spiraling horns of rams comprise up to 13 percent of their bodyweight.

NORTH AMERICAN BEAVER

Castor canadensis
Family: CASTORIDAE
Order: RODENTIA

DISTRIBUTION: Small lakes and streams among light woodland in Canada, Alaska and much of coterminous United States. The species has also been introduced to parts of Finland.

SIZE: Length 32–47in (0.8–1.2m); height 12–23in (30–60cm); tail 10–20in (25–50cm); weight 24–66lb (11–30kg).

APPEARANCE: A large robust rodent with short legs and large, webbed hind feet. The tail is flattened like a paddle and covered in scaly skin. The face is small and neat with small eyes and ears and long orange upper incisor teeth. The coat is dense, waterproof and fawn to chocolate brown in color.

DIET: Aquatic plants such as water lilies, plus the leaves, bark, twigs, roots of waterside trees and shrubs.

BREEDING: Females give birth to one litter of up to 2–4 young in spring, after a 100–110 day gestation. The cubs are weaned at 3 months, and remain with their parents until they become sexually mature at 18–24 months. Beavers can live up to 24 years in the wild.

LIFESTYLE: Beaver colonies comprise small territorial family groups with one breeding pair. Beavers mate for life and all members of the family help with chores such as maintaining the home, and feeding and caring for the young. They communicate using various hisses and grunts and advertise their presence by slapping their flat tail on the water. They use dung and heaps of dirt and twigs scented with a musky secretion called castoreum to mark out their territory.

Beavers are semi-aquatic and largely nocturnal, but their prodigious construction abilities make them highly conspicuous. Firstly they dam up a stream, using branches and sometimes whole trees felled by their chisel-like front teeth and transported across the water. The dam creates a large pool in which the beavers then build a lodge – a mound of timber and silt containing a living chamber with an underwater entrance hole.

Beavers do not hibernate, but in severe winters they are often sealed in to their lodge pools by a thick layer of ice. They survive on plant material stored in special caches during summer.

BEAVERS ON THE BRINK
American beavers were ruthlessly exploited by fur trappers throughout the 18th and 19th centuries. Annual catches of 100,000 animals were not uncommon. Rivalry between France and England over the fur trade even led to war. The species was almost driven to extinction before strict trapping regulations were introduced.

MUSKRAT

Ondatra zibethicus
Family: MURIDAE
Order: RODENTIA

DISTRIBUTION: The common muskrat lives in well-vegetated pools, lakes, rivers, marshes, and swamps from (mostly) Southern Canada, through most of the coterminous United States (not California, Texas or Florida), to Baja California in Mexico. Introduced populations in Eurasia and South America are regarded as pests. Hunting for fur has declined since the early 1970s and the species is not currently threatened.

SIZE: This mammal is the largest member of the mouse and vole family. Length 9–13in (23–32cm); tail 7–11.5in (18–30cm); weight 1.5–4lb (0.68–1.8kg).

APPEARANCE: A large rat-like animal with a slightly flattened, rudder-like tail and large, partially webbed hind feet. The feet bear a fringe of stiff hairs on the outer edges, which improve swimming efficiency. The fur is glossy and ranges from dark- or silvery-brown to black.

DIET: Aquatic plants, grasses and some animal matter.

A VOLE NOT A RAT
Muskrats are not really rats at all, but a kind of large vole. They feed mostly on water plants, which they gather underwater and manipulate using their nimble front paws.

BREEDING: Females can deliver up to 50 young a year. Litter sizes vary from 1–11, being generally smaller but more numerous in the south. Gestation lasts 25–30 days and weaning happens between 2 and 3 weeks. Southern muskrats mature as early as 6–8 weeks, development is slower in the north. Longevity is up to 10 years, but averages less than 5.

LIFESTYLE: Muskrats always live close to water. Burrows are dug directly into the banks of rivers and canals, with entrances well below the water level. In swamps and marshes where there are few banks, the muskrats construct a mound of rotted plant material and mud with a nest chamber inside and an underwater entrance. Muskrats are most active between dusk and dawn. They are excellent swimmers and collect most of their food underwater. They can remain submerged for up to 15 minutes at a time. The species lives alone or in small colonies of related animals. They are rather bad tempered and members of a colony will repel intruders aggressively. They make few sounds, but will growl when annoyed.

SIBERIAN CHIPMUNK

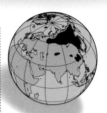

Tamias sibiricus
Family: SCIURIDAE
Order: RODENTIA

DISTRIBUTION: In forests from northeastern Europe through Siberia, Mongolia, northern and central China to Korea and also in Japan.

SIZE: Length 4.5–6.7in (12–17cm); tail 3–4.5in (8–11.5cm); weight 1.75–4.2oz (50–120g).

APPEARANCE: A small squirrel with a large head and a long, thin, furry tail. The coat is brownish or yellowish gray and there are two dark lines down each flank separated by a third stripe of bright white fur.

DIET: Siberian chipmunks eat predominantly seeds and nuts, with some fruit, grains, fungi, and animal matter.

BREEDING: Adult chipmunks mate soon after waking from hibernation and litters of 3–7 young are born about a month later in May–June. In warmer southern parts of the range there may be time to rear a second litter before the onset of winter. The youngsters are weaned at 50–57 days and must then collect enough food to see themselves though the winter. They reach sexual maturity the following spring and usually live between 2 and 4 years.

LIFESTYLE: Siberian chipmunks are active for just six months of every year and spend most of their summers busily collecting food. They are agile climbers and will forage in trees as well as on the ground. They accumulate far more than they can actually eat, and stash it away in numerous stores. The Siberian chipmunk's burrow usually has at least 2 chambers, one for sleeping and the other to serve as a larder. Additional food is buried beneath the leaf litter outside the burrow. The animals make use of the long summer days gathering food and sleep at night. Hibernation begins in October or November. The chipmunk enters a deep sleep, and both its body temperature and metabolic rate drop significantly. There is usually a period of wakefulness in midwinter, when the animal makes use of stored food, before going back to sleep until spring.

Siberian chipmunks are territorial. Females have larger territories than males – up to one acre (0.5ha) in some places.

LISTEN OUT
Siberian chipmunks often pause in their foraging activities to call and listen out for the calls of other chipmunks. The calls are high-pitched chirps and twitters.

AMERICAN RED SQUIRREL

Tamaisciurus hudsonicus
Family: SCIURIDAE
Order: RODENTIA

DISTRIBUTION: Mixed, coniferous and deciduous woodland throughout temperate Canada and Alaska and in mountainous regions of North America including the Rocky and Appalachian ranges.

SIZE: Length 6.5–9in (16.5–23cm); tail 3.5–6.2in (9–16cm); weight 5–11oz (140–310g).

APPEARANCE: A dainty squirrel with reddish-brown fur and a white chest. In summer there is a dark stripe down each flank. The tail is less bushy than in other American squirrels and is sometimes fringed with white. A ring of white around each eye makes them look large.

DIET: Pine cones, nuts, seeds, fruit, bark, sap, fungi, and some animal matter.

BREEDING: Canadian red squirrels usually breed just once a year. Those further south often manage to rear 2 litters of 2–6 babies in spring and mid summer. The young are born after a gestation lasting about 34 days and are weaned at 7–10 weeks. Most breed themselves the following year. Potential longevity is as much as 10 years, but 7 is more normal in the wild.

LIFESTYLE: The American red squirrel has a relatively lightweight body that allows it to venture to the tips of slender branches. It is an accomplished climber, but also spends time on the ground, foraging for fallen nuts, fungi, and insects in the leaf litter. The species has a well-organized approach to foraging. Individuals harvest the sweet sap of maple trees over a period of days by first making a deep cut in the bark, then returning later to collect the syrupy blob that has leaked out. Like other squirrels they store large quantities of food to act as a winter larder.

Red squirrels use a variety of chattering and buzzing sounds to

warn off intruders from their
territory. Adults usually build
several different nests within their
home range and use them at
different times of year. Winter
nests are usually in tree holes or
dense thickets, or sometimes below
the ground. Summer nests are built
in more exposed locations, out on
the branches of trees where they
are well ventilated and cool and
difficult for most predators to
reach. Young squirrels disperse in
search of their own territories at
about 18 weeks old, and
sometimes the mother will move on
too, leaving a vacant range for at
least one of her offspring.

SECRET STORE
Red squirrels are
territorial. They
defend a small area
of good foraging
habitat all year
round and in winter
will protect the areas
around their food
store from other
squirrels.

WOODCHUCK

Marmota monax
Family: SCIURIDAE
Order: RODENTIA

DISTRIBUTION: Prairie regions of North America from Alaska and Newfoundland south to Idaho and Alabama. Range expanded as previously unsuitable habitat was developed for agriculture but hunting and persecution have since caused declines in some areas.

SIZE: Length 16–26in (40.5–66cm); tail 4–10in (10–25cm); weight 4.4–13.2lb (2–6kg).

APPEARANCE: A robust, short-legged, short-tailed rodent. The legs are short and powerful and bear strong claws to help loosen packed soil, which is then shoved back by the soles of the woodchuck's flat feet. The fur is dense, woolly and reddish brown with white-tipped guard hairs. The face is squirrel like, with small eyes and small rounded ears.

DIET: Large quantities of fresh green vegetation, also seeds and fruit. Woodchucks can become pests by raiding crops such as alfalfa, corn and oats.

BREEDING: Litters of 1–9 (usually 4 or 5) young are born once a year in spring after 30–32 days gestation. The babies are suckled for 6 weeks. Woodchucks are sexually mature at 2 years and may live up to 6 years in the wild.

LIFESTYLE: The American woodchuck is a highly proficient digger. Its burrows may be up to 50 feet (15m) long and have 4 or 5 entrances. Different dens are used at different times of year. Summer burrows are dug in open ground and marked by a heap of fresh dirt at the entrance. Winter dens are less obvious and are usually excavated among tree roots, which help prevent collapses as the ground becomes soggier.

Woodchucks usually live alone, but territory sizes vary with habitat and season. Breeding females can use as little as a half an acre (0.25ha) while males defend up to 7.5 acres (3ha) of personal space. Males and females use scent and a variety of vocalizations to mark out their personal territory and intruders, including newly independent juveniles, are scolded and driven away with aggressive chattering. Woodchucks spend the winter in hibernation, living off reserves of body fat for several months and usually emerging some time in March or April.

WHISTLEPIG
Woodchucks are alert and nervous animals. This is a typical lookout posture. On detecting a threat, they issue a high-pitched and far-carrying alarm call, hence their alternative name "whistlepig."

ALPINE MARMOT

Marmota marmota
Family: SCIURIDAE
Order: CARNIVORA

DISTRIBUTION: Mountain meadows and rocky slopes in alpine regions of Italy, France, and Switzerland. The species has been reintroduced to places where the fossil record indicates it once occurred naturally, including the Pyrenees, the Carpathians, and Germany's Black Forest.

SIZE: Length 18–20in (47–52cm); tail 6–8in (15–20cm); weight 6–10lb (2.8–4.5kg).

APPEARANCE: A short-tailed, chunky squirrel with short muscular legs and a coat of golden brown to gray fur.

DIET: Grasses, herbs, roots, fruit, and flowers.

BREEDING: Marmots breed once a year. Litters of 2–6 young are born in May–June after 34 days gestation. The young are weaned at 40 days, and are sexually mature at 18 months. They may live up to 15 years.

LIFESTYLE: Alpine marmots are highly social. They live in family groups in extensive burrow systems. There is a lot of close physical contact, including nuzzling and mutual grooming and the marmots communicate using a variety of sounds, the most commonly heard of which is a shrill warning whistle. Only one dominant female is allowed to breed, usually with the dominant male, but occasionally she will mate with one of her sons or with an unrelated visiting male. The breeding male is responsible for defending the territory. Other members of the group (usually the offspring of the last two or three summers) help rear the young and keep them warm in winter.

Marmots forage for green shoots within a home range of up to 11 acres (4.5ha). They have excellent vision and hearing and a keen sense of smell. They use saliva to mark their territory.

In winter suitable food is scarce and the marmots are forced to hibernate in order to conserve energy. Hibernation lasts 6–7 months and happens in a chamber blocked up with grass and dirt for security and warmth.

In midsummer, marmots' daytime activities are restricted to morning and afternoon to avoid the heat of the midday sun. They do not cope well with hot weather, though on cool clear mornings they will bask outside their burrows.

ON GUARD
When the Alpine marmot's territory is threatened, it will adopt a vigilant upright posture and give a shrill whistle of alarm.

HOUSE MOUSE

Mus musculus
Family: MURIDAE
Order: RODENTIA

DISTRIBUTION: Worldwide wherever people dwell or work (in farms, food stores, and fields).

SIZE: Length 3–4.5in (7–10cm); tail 3–4in (7–8.5cm); weight 0.5–1oz (12–22g)

APPEARANCE: Small slim mouse with a pointed face, small beady eyes and large round ears. The tail is long with scaly pink skin showing through very sparse hairs. The fur on the rest of the body is grayish-brown and often greasy looking.

DIET: House mice can make a meal out if almost anything organic. They prefer seeds and grains, but will eat anything humans do, and all kinds of plant and animal material including leather, wood, wax, cloth, soap, and paper. They also chew synthetic materials such as plastics and man-made fabrics.

BREEDING: House mice breed extremely fast. Females are sexually mature at six weeks and can produce up to 14 litters of

4–10 young a year. Gestation takes just 19–21 days for first litters, a little more if the female is still suckling a previous litter. The young are weaned at 3 weeks and independent at 5 or 6 weeks. Mice can live up to 6 years in captivity, but rarely over 2 years in the wild.

LIFESTYLE: House mice rarely live together in large numbers in the wild, and they do not usually defend territories. When forced to live alongside many other mice, however, as in barns and farm stores, they will compete aggressively for a bit of personal space. Some territories are very small and where food is plentiful, as in grain stores, established mice may never travel more than a few feet from their nests. Males fight for dominance over one another, but will permit females to live with them. Both females and young mice help defend the family territory. Young mice disperse soon to new ranges before they begin breeding themselves. This helps prevent inbreeding and is one of the main reasons house mice populations spread so quickly. The other is of course that the species reproduces very rapidly.

PEST PROBLEM
House mice are regarded as pests because they spoil food, leave droppings in houses, and eat through anything such as wires.

HARVEST MOUSE

Micromys minutus
Family: MURIDAE
Order: RODENTIA

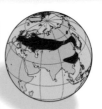

DISTRIBUTION: Grasslands, meadows, fields, thickets and reed beds of Europe and Asia from Western Europe eastwards to Siberia, Korea and China. Also on Taiwan and in Japan. The species is declining as a result of modern farming practices.

SIZE: One of the world's smallest rodents. Length 2–3in (5–7.5cm); tail 2–3in (5–7.5cm); weight 0.2–0.25oz (5–7g).

APPEARANCE: A tiny mouse with golden brown fur and a white underside. The tail is long, thin and semi-prehensile, with a patch of hairless skin near the tip that helps grip plant stems when climbing. Juveniles are grayish.

DIET: Seeds, buds, fruits, and green shoots.

BREEDING: Several litters of 1–13 (usually 3–5) young are born in spring and summer after a 17–18 day gestation. They are weaned at 2 weeks and leave the nest soon after. Harvest mice rarely live longer than 18 months.

LIFESTYLE: Harvest mice are secretive, mostly nocturnal and very small. Often the only obvious clue to their presence is a collection of baseball-sized nests intricately woven from shredded grass among tall stems or tucked away in a tussock, hedgerow or at the base of a shrub such as blackthorn. The nests have a small entrance on the underside, but this is usually concealed while the nest is in use. There may be several such nests within a home range. The mice are agile climbers and will ascend into trees and shrubs in search of flowers and seeds.

Harvest mice are generally solitary and as the breeding season approaches male especially become aggressively territorial. In winter they become much more tolerant of each other and often

NOT SO TIMID
A male harvest mouse's advances are rebuffed by the female. Rivalry between male harvest mice peaks during the spring, when they vie for territories that will give them access to females.

several individuals will live in close proximity in a refuge such as a tree hole, abandoned burrow or a hay barn. Harvest mice are vulnerable to a wide range of predators including mammals and birds. They are generally nocturnal but may avoid coming out on bright moonlit nights.

BROWN RAT

Rattus norvegicus
Family: MURIDAE
Order: RODENTIA

DISTRIBUTION: Worldwide in virtually all habitats.

SIZE: Length 8.5–11.5in (21.5–29cm); tail 6.5–9in (17–23cm); weight 9–28oz (250–800g).

APPEARANCE: Highly familiar shape to humans (with whom it has a long association) with a robust, cylindrical body, long scaly tail and pointed face. The short legs have longish fingers and toes and the fur is a dull grayish brown, fading to white or pale gray on the belly. The ears are rounded and prominent, the eyes are bright and beady.

DIET: Rats eat anything from fruit, grain, and eggs to wax, leather, paper, and soap. They prefer meat, catching other small animals to eat.

BREEDING: In theory, under ideal conditions, a single pair of brown rats can multiply to over 10,000 animals in the space of a year. Females begin breeding at 2–3 months of age and can then rear up to 12 litters of 1–22 (usually 8 or 9) young a year. Gestation lasts 21–26 days and the litters can be weaned at 3 weeks. Few wild brown rats survive more than 3 years, though captives may live twice as long.

LIFESTYLE: Prior to their association with people, brown rats probably lived in stream banks, and they have retained a liking for damp places. They are excellent swimmers and can even catch fish. They are also effective diggers and where they still live outside they build extensive burrow systems. They are reasonably agile, but generally prefer to live and forage at ground level.

The way groups and individual brown rats interact depends on population density. At low densities, dominant males defend territories containing several females, which cooperate to rear his offspring. Where overcrowding precludes such organization, males are nonterritorial but must fight instead for every female.

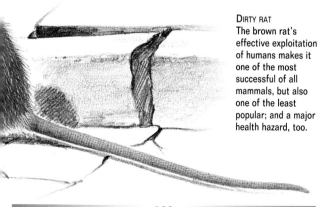

DIRTY RAT
The brown rat's effective exploitation of humans makes it one of the most successful of all mammals, but also one of the least popular; and a major health hazard, too.

NORWAY LEMMING

Lemmus lemmus
Family: MURIDAE
Order: RODENTIA

DISTRIBUTION: Tundra of Norway, Sweden, Finland and extreme northwestern Russia. Lives under snow for half the year, makes extraordinary mass migrations when population explodes.

SIZE: Length 3–6in (7–15.5cm); tail 0.5in (1–2cm); weight: 0.5–5oz (15–130g).

APPEARANCE: Rounded body and head, and very short tail. The coat is very thick to cope with the Arctic winters and boldly colored with creamy yellow on the belly, reddish brown on the back, and almost brownish-black on the shoulders, head, and face. The lemming has small inconspicuous ears, bright eyes, and long whiskers. The thumb of each front foot bears a large, flat claw for shovelling snow.

DIET: Herbivorous: mostly mosses, also leaves and shoots of grasses and sedges, lichen, fruit, and bark collected at ground level using network of snow tunnels in winter.

BREEDING: Among the world's fastest breeding mammals. Up to 6 litters of 1–13 (usually 5–8) young usually born in spring and summer after 16–23 day gestation. Under ideal conditions females may breed every 21 days all year round, leading to "boom and bust" population cycle. At the peak of a population cycle, there may be 100 lemmings per acre (250 per hectare).Young weaned at 14–16 days, females sexually mature at just 2–3 weeks, males at 3–4 weeks. Individuals rarely live more than 2 years.

LIFESTYLE: Lemmings are busy little animals, active day and night all year around. They are also highly unsociable and meetings between neighbors usually trigger angry squeaking and fights. They spend most of their lives in burrows under the ground or tunnels in the snow, emerging only to collect food or sometimes to migrate. The burrows have several chambers, some for storing food and others for use as latrines. Breeding and sleeping chambers have snug nests of grass and fur.

Lemming migrations are legendary. Sometimes thousands of animals travel together, often at breakneck speed and seemingly reckless of their own safety.

However stories of mass-suicides where thousands of lemmings hurl themselves over cliffs are exaggerated. In reality the migrations are the result of overcrowding due to sudden population booms. Such increases usually follow mild winters, which allow breeding to continue throughout the year. For such aggressive and antisocial animals, overcrowding is intolerable and the migrations are an attempt to find better conditions elsewhere.

SNOWED UNDER
Norway lemmings are among the world's hardiest mammals. They spend half the year living under several feet of snow in almost total darkness. They do not hibernate.

EUROPEAN WATER VOLE

Arvicola terrestris
Family: MURIDAE
Order: RODENTIA

DISTRIBUTION: Widespread throughout most of central and eastern Europe including Great Britain and Scandinavia, east through Siberia to Mongolia. Water voles inhabit the banks of freshwater streams and rivers, and may also live away from water in meadows and pastures.

SIZE: Length 4.5–9in (12–23cm); tail 1.5–5.5in (4–14cm); weight 3–11oz (80–320g). There is considerable geographic variation in size; northern specimens grow much bigger than southern ones.

APPEARANCE: A chubby, ratlike rodent with a rounded head and body, a blunt face and a thin, scaly tail. The fur is thick and brown.

DIET: Mostly grasses, sedges, and roots, occasionally small fish and other aquatic animals.

BREEDING: Voles breed in summer, and females over the age of 11 or 12 months rear 2–5 litters of 2–8 (usually 4–6 young) a year. The gestation period is 20–22 days and young are suckled for just 2–3 weeks. Longevity is up to 5 years in captivity, rarely more than 18 months in the wild.

LIFESTYLE: Water voles are traditionally thought of as semiaquatic animals of the riverbank. However in parts of eastern Europe and Siberia, they

are often found living well away from rivers, in fields and grasslands. Here they spend much of their lives underground, feeding on roots and bulbs. In some places they damage crops and are regarded as a pest. Elsewhere, they build nests in holes in river banks, usually with at least one entrance under water. Water voles are proficient swimmers, both at the surface and underwater. Their hind feet bear a short swimming fringe, but there is no webbing between the toes.

Voles are active day and night. Much of their waking hours are spent foraging, but during the spring and summer breeding season they also spend much time marking and defending territory. Males defend a stretch of bank about 330–660 feet (100–200m) long, and their territories overlap with the smaller ranges of females. During the winter hostilities are suspended and many voles share a burrow, huddling together for warmth. They are active all winter, sometimes relying on stored grass and other food to survive severe weather when they cannot forage.

A WATERY ESCAPE Water voles usually drop into the water with a loud "plop!" whenever they hear something approaching.

COMMON HAMSTER

Cricetus cricetus
Family: MURIDAE
Order: RODENTIA

DISTRIBUTION: Central and eastern Europe, western and central Asia as far as Altai mountains in Siberia. Hamsters occupy steppe grassland and farmland and are also often found on riverbanks.

SIZE: Length 8–13in (20–34cm); tail 1.5–2.5in (4–6cm); weight 4–31oz (110–900g).

APPEARANCE: A large rodent with a short, naked tail and large feet. The fur coloration is unusual, being light brown on the head and back, with white patches on the chin, throat, and flanks and almost black on the belly. The feet are white. The cheek pouches, when full, expand to the size of the head.

DIET: Seeds, grains, beans, and pulses, plus roots, shoots, leaves, and some animal material, mainly insect larvae and small amphibians.

BREEDING: Females mature at 6–7 weeks and can rear young at any time of year. Gestation lasts 18–20 days and litters contain anywhere between 4 and 12 young, which are fully weaned at 3 weeks old. The potential for fast breeding is balanced by a short life, rarely more than 2 years.

LIFESTYLE: Far from the cute and cuddly image of pet hamsters, wild common hamsters are solitary and aggressive animals. They live alone in a self-dug burrow, which they continue to extend, modify, and guard throughout life. Males and females come together only briefly for mating, and the male is driven away again immediately afterward.

In spring and summer, individuals emerge at dusk and dawn to forage. Nonperishable foods such as grains and dried peas are carried back to the burrow and stored in specially constructed larders. Some hamster burrows have been found to contain almost 200 pounds (90kg) of stored food.

These stores are an insurance policy against harsh winters during which the hamsters cannot forage. The animals hibernate in late fall and wake up once every week to feed. They are not as dependent on accumulated body fat as are many other hibernators.

CHEEKY FEEDERS
Hamsters collect far more food than they can actually eat and stuff the excess into a pair of large pouches inside their cheeks.

MONGOLIAN GERBIL

Meriones unguioculatus
Family: MURIDAE
Order: RODENTIA

DISTRIBUTION: Dry grassland, steppe, and desert regions of Mongolia, southern Siberia and northern China.

SIZE: Length 4–5in (10–12.5cm); tail 3.8–4.4in (9.5–11cm); weight 2.5–4.6oz (70–130g).

APPEARANCE: A small, sand-colored rodent with a long, furry tail with a dark brushy tip. The hind feet are long, and all toes have long claws. The eyes are large, the ears small but prominent and there may be light markings on the face.

DIET: All kinds of plant material including seeds, leaves, shoots, roots, fruit; also eats insects.

BREEDING: Up to 3 litters of 4–7 young are born in spring, summer or fall after a 19–21 day gestation. They are weaned at 3 weeks and ready to breed at 15 weeks. Potential longevity is 4 years, though wild specimens rarely survive longer than 2 years.

LIFESTYLE: Gerbils (or jirds, as they are more properly known) are desert specialists. Their soft, slightly shaggy coat provides good camouflage as well as insulation against heat and cold. Despite having to endure extremes of temperature and perpetual drought, gerbils are active all year round. Large quantities of foods such as seeds and grains are stored in special larders as a contingency against seasonal food shortage.

Mongolian jirds live in shallow, multi-chambered burrows, which they usually share with several other individuals of either sex. Males and females both help care for the young, but unusually, adult gerbils appear more likely to share this responsibility with a sibling than a mate. Females mate with unrelated males living nearby before returning to their own home burrow, where the young will be tended to by their uncle instead of their father. Adults and young use various squeaks and foot drumming for communication. Mongolian jirds are very active, and may wander more than half a mile a day in search of food. On leaving the nest, young animals have been known to disperse 30 miles (50km) or more before they settle. Gerbils have many predators and are nervous when moving above ground. At the slightest hint of danger they sprint for cover and the dark tipped tail is thought to serve as a decoy, diverting attention from the animal's head.

POPULAR PET
The Mongolian gerbil, also known as the jird, is a popular children's pet. Its clean habits and social nature make it easy to care for in captivity, and being active in the daytime it is most active when its owner is awake to enjoy its antics. It also does not hibernate in winter, but In the wild it may spend long periods without emerging above ground, living on stored food.

COMMON DORMOUSE

Muscardinus avellanarius
Family: MYOXIDAE
Order: RODENTIA

DISTRIBUTION: Woodland with thickets of nut-bearing trees such as hazel in southern and western Great Britain and most of west and central mainland Europe except northern Scandinavia, Iberia, and the low countries.

SIZE: Length 2.5–3.5in (6–9cm); tail 2–3in (5.5–7.5cm); weight 0.5–1.4oz (15–40g).

APPEARANCE: A small, very appealing mouse with a long furry tail. The fur is golden and quite thick and the face is short with bright black eyes, small ears, and long whiskers.

DIET: Mostly nuts, seeds, flowers, and buds, fruit, and insects and occasionally eggs and baby birds.

BREEDING: 1 or 2 litters of 2–7 (usually 3–5) young are born in midsummer after a 22–24 day gestation. The young are weaned at about 40 days and reach sexual maturity after their first hibernation

at about 11 months. Wild dormice may live up to 5 years.

LIFESTYLE: The common dormouse is secretive and difficult to see in the wild. It is active only at night, usually amid dense vegetation above ground level. In winter it hibernates for 6 or 7 months, tucked away in a burrow or among tree roots. This hibernation is very deep – the dormouse's body temperature drops as low as one fourth of a degree above freezing and its heart and breathing rate are reduced to a bare minimum. Only by taking such extreme energy-saving measures can the animal make its limited reserves of fat last. It cannot afford to wake up before spring because of the extra energy it requires to warm its body and kick start its metabolism. Over wintering dormice usually lose about one third of their body weight.

Dormice make up for the months

of inactivity by packing an entire year's worth of activity into 5 months in summer. During this time they feed, build breeding nests, find a mate and produce young. Summer nests are woven from strips of honeysuckle and other fine vegetation. Dormice are sociable, and their nests are usually built in clusters. The young often remain together after their mother has abandoned them at about 40 days.

CONFIDENT CLIMBER
Dormice are nimble and confident climbers. Their feet have long toes and thick pads to provide grip. The long, furry tail serves as a counterbalance.

NORTH AMERICAN PORCUPINE

Erethizon dorsatum
Family: ERETHIZONTIDAE
Order: RODENTIA

DISTRIBUTION: Occupies mixed forest and other well vegetated habitats throughout North America, from Alaska south to northern Mexico and the Carolinas.

SIZE: Length 25–34in (64–86cm); tail 5.5–12in (14.5–30cm); weight 7.7–40lb (3.5–18kg).

APPEARANCE: A large rodent covered in stiff, brown to black fur interspersed with yellow quills. The quills are actually enlarged hairs. Those on the rump are very long, while short spines grow hidden among the fur everywhere else except on the belly. The face is short, with small dark eyes and small inconspicuous ears. The porcupine's feet have naked soles and long, thick claws.

DIET: All kinds of plant material including leaves and shoots, buds, flowers, fruit, seeds, nuts, twigs, bark and soft wood. Also gnaw bones to extract calcium and minerals and sharpen their teeth.

BREEDING: Porcupines breed slowly. Precocious young are born in spring, usually just one at a time after 7.5 months gestation. They are fully furred, with open eyes and are able to walk and climb almost immediately. Weaning happens at just 2–6 weeks, but it takes 2 years to reach sexual maturity. Some individuals live as long as 18 years.

LIFESTYLE: Intelligent animals with sharp senses and good memories, porcupines are generally nocturnal and spend most of their time in the branches of trees. When threatened, a porcupine turns its back and raises its quills. It thrashes its short tail at its enemy. The quills detach easily from the porcupine's skin and their barbed tips allow them to slip painfully into the flesh. Of the few predators that manage to hunt porcupines, most have learned the knack of flipping them over and attacking the

unprotected belly. Adult porcupines usually live alone. Home ranges are larger in summer when the porcupines wander widely in search of the most nutritious fruits, seeds, bulbs and tubers. In winter they go for quantity not quality, eating readily available but less nutritious pine needles and soft woody tissues and rarely venturing far from the den.

TREE CLIMBER
Porcupines are excellent climbers and move about the branches of trees with cautious but confident movements. Their long claws and naked soles and palms provide good grip.

CAPYBARA

Hydrochaeris hydrochaeris
Family: HYDROCHAERIDAE
Order: RODENTIA

DISTRIBUTION: Grassland and forest alongside rivers and pools in South America. The range extends south from Panama and east from the Andes mountains, and includes parts of Colombia, Venezuela, Brazil, Paraguay and northern Argentina. Numbers decreased rapidly in the past because of hunting for their meat and hides. They are ranched in some areas.

SIZE: The world's largest rodent. Length 42–53in (1.1–1.34m); height 20–24in (50–62cm); weight 77–146lb (35–66kg).

APPEARANCE: A tall, tailless rodent with a barrel-body and slender legs. The fur is sparse and reddish brown, the head is large with a deep muzzle. The nostrils, ears and eyes are located high on the head so the animal can breathe, hear and see while swimming low in the water. The feet are partially webbed. Males have a large gland on the top of snout, known as the morillo.

DIET: Grasses and aquatic plants.

BREEDING: Females first breed at 12 months and give birth to 1 or 2 litters of 1–8 (usually 3–5) precocious young a year, usually in the wet season. Courtship and mating happen in the water. Gestation lasts 150 days and the babies are reared communally. Females will suckle one another's young, but weaning begins almost immediately.

LIFESTYLE: The scientific name *Hydrochaeris* means "water-pig", but the capybara is in fact a large rodent. Capybaras are excellent swimmers and spend most of their active lives close to water, though feeding takes place on the banks. They live in family groups, comprising one dominant breeding male, one or more females and their young, and sometimes a number of young subordinate males. Members of the colony recognize each other by smell and use scent to mark a joint territory, 5 to 500 acres (2–200ha) in area. In the dry season several colonies may form a large temporary herd, which migrates in search of water and breaks up again as soon as conditions improve.

Capybaras produce two kinds of droppings. The first are soft and green and still contain nutrients after one passage through the digestive system. These are reingested and passed though the gut once more. The second droppings are hard and dry and contain only true waste.

WATER HAVEN
On land the capybara is rather clumsy and slow, but is capable of short dashes to the safety of water. This is enough to deter most land-based predators such as jaguars, foxes, and vultures. However, young capybaras are known to come under attack in the water from caimans and bush dogs.

GUINEA PIG

Cavia porcellus
Family: CAVIIDAE
Order: RODENTIA

Possible range of
feral populations

DISTRIBUTION: Guinea pigs originally lived wild in South America, from central Ecuador east to Suriname and south to Peru, Uruguay and northern Argentina in grassland and forest margins. Subsequently they were farmed extensively throughout the Andean region and many populations are now considered feral. The species tolerates a wide range of habitat and climate types, but individuals do not cope well with sudden change.

SIZE: Length 8–12in (20–30cm); there is no tail; weight 18–21oz (500–600g).

APPEARANCE: A neat-looking animal with a rat-like body, the guinea pig has very short legs and no tail. The head is relatively large with small ears and beady eyes. The coat is short and glossy and very variable in color and pattern. Wild guinea pigs are generally smaller and slimmer than their domestic counterparts.

DIET: Leaves, shoots, seeds, grains and other plant material. The young are weaned onto plant food by first eating their mother's fresh green droppings which contain both nutrients and vital gut-dwelling bacteria.

BREEDING: Females can rear several litters of up to a dozen young at any time of year, but not in severe winters. Gestation lasts about 2 months and the babies grow fast. They are weaned at 3 weeks and sexually mature at 2 months. Under favorable conditions they may live up to 8 years.

LIFESTYLE: This species is one of three possible ancestors of the domestic guinea pig and experts are divided as to whether any populations now exist in a truly wild state.

Where they are allowed to live wild, guinea pigs are cautious, nocturnal, ground-dwelling animals.

They are not particularly quick or agile, and their noisy babbling and chattering calls have earned them an undeserved reputation for stupidity.

Wild guinea pigs live in small groups of up to 10 individuals, sleeping and sheltering in burrows or thick scrub. They are generally peaceful and non-territorial, but each sex has a distinct dominance hierarchy and males will fight for superiority, especially in the presence of a female on heat.

Guinea pigs coats come in a wide variety of colors and patterns.

Some of this variability is natural, but some of the more striking patterns are almost certainly the result of selective breeding of domestic ancestors.

SOUTH AMERICAN FOOD SOURCE
The name guinea pig refers to the domesticated form of the cavy (*Cavia porcellus*). Cavies are widely kept and traded in the Andean region of South America, where they make ideal livestock for smallholders seeking a food resource.

CHINCHILLA

Chinchilla lanigera
Family: CHINCHILLIDAE
Order: RODENTIA

DISTRIBUTION: The wild chinchilla is found on the rocky slopes of the Andes mountains in southern Peru, Bolivia, northern Chile and northern Argentina. The species suffered greatly from excessive trapping for fur, and despite protection there are less than 10,000 left in the wild. Many more live in captivity.

SIZE: Length 9–15in (22.5–38cm); tail 3–6in (7.5–15cm); weight 14–28oz (400-800g).

APPEARANCE: A cuddly-looking rodent with a bushy tail and short front legs – the hind limbs are longer. Most distinctive is the amazingly soft, silvery-gray fur. With up to 60 hairs growing from each follicle, this is among the finest and densest of all mammal coats. The chinchilla's head is rather large with big round eyes, large oval ears and long whiskers.

DIET: Chinchillas will eat almost any available vegetation.

BREEDING: Young chinchillas are born large and very well developed in litters of 1 to 6 between May and November, after a long gestation (111 days). They are suckled for 6 to 8 weeks and are ready to breed at 8 months. Captives have lived as long as 20 years, but 10 is a good age in the wild.

LIFESTYLE: In the wild chinchillas live in barren regions in holes and crevices among rocks and come out at dusk to forage for what vegetation there is. Although chinchillas are nocturnal, they may remain outside on sunny days, basking in the sun close to their burrow entrances. At night they rely on their exceptional fur for warmth in the thin, often icy mountain air.

Chinchillas are social rodents and while large colonies are probably a thing of the past most live in mixed groups of a dozen or more.

Females in heat are aggressive, but for most of the year these are tolerant animals. It is said that despite their nervous disposition, chinchillas are insatiably curious – one of the traits that made them so tragically vulnerable to trapping. They are also agile rock climbers, using their long hind legs for leaping. Anyone who has held a pet chinchilla will understand why their fur is so prized.

CONSTANT MONITOR
Chinchillas are alert, easily unsettled, and capable of moving extremely fast. Their large eyes provide excellent vision and the large ears swivel constantly to monitor for signs of danger.

EUROPEAN RABBIT

Oryctolagus cuniculus
Family: LEPORIDAE
Order: LAGOMORPHA

DISTRIBUTION: Rabbits are native to the Iberian Peninsula and southern France, but thrive as introduced animals in grassland and agricultural habitats throughout Europe and northern Africa, and in Australia and New Zealand. The species' success is often in spite of intensive eradication efforts by humans.

SIZE: Length 15–20in (35–50cm); tail 1.5–3in (4.5–7.5cm); weight 3–6.6lb (1.35–3kg).

APPEARANCE: A small, stout animal with long, powerful back legs and a short, fluffy tail. The head is very round with large bulging eyes and long, erect, oval ears. The fur is dense and very soft, usually grayish brown to black, and paler on the under parts.

DIET: Grass, also stems and leaves of all kinds of other plants. In winter rabbits can survive on the soft woody tissues of trees and shrubs, stripped out from under the bark.

BREEDING: A healthy female can breed from the age of 3 months and can rear 7 litters of 1–9 (usually 5 or 6) young in a season, mating almost immediately after giving birth and weaning one litter just in time to make way for the next. The young are left alone for long periods in the nest chamber. The mother visits just once a day to suckle them, to avoid attracting attention to their location. Individuals rarely live longer than 10 years in the wild.

LIFESTYLE: Unlike other rabbits, the European species does well in open spaces thanks to its prodigious skill at burrowing. Burrows range from short, blind-ending tunnels to huge, complicated warrens covering 2.5 acres (1ha) or more and containing hundreds of animals. There is a strict hierarchy among the adult rabbits in a colony. Rank determines which males mate with most females and which females get the best nest sites. Breeding groups usually include one to four adult males and up to 9 breeding females. Aggression is quite common, especially between females. Young male rabbits disperse from the home warren as juveniles, while females do so only occasionally.

24/7 MAMMALS
Rabbits are hardy animals and cope well with a variety of seasonal climates, remaining active all year round. They are most active around dawn and dusk but can be out an about at any time of day or night.

EASTERN COTTONTAIL

Sylvilagus floridanus
Family: LEPORIDAE
Order: LAGOMORPHA

DISTRIBUTION: Eastern North America from southern Manitoba, Ontario, and Quebec in Canada, through eastern and Midwestern United States and Central America to Colombia and Venezuela. Cottontails occupy a wide range of habitats from forests and scrub to swamps and meadows.

SIZE: Length 10–18in (30–47cm); tail 1–2.5in (2.5–6cm); weight 1.8–4lb (0.9–1.8kg).

APPEARANCE: A large rabbit with dense, soft, woolly gray-brown fur and a white powder puff tail. The head is small and rounded with long oval ears and bright, slightly bulging eyes.

DIET: Grasses and herbaceous plants in summer; twigs, buds, and bark in winter.

BREEDING: 3–4 litters of 2–12 are born between spring and early fall after a 26–32 day gestation. The young are reared in a succession of nests, the mother moves them around frequently and suckles them once a day but otherwise spends as little time with them as possible in order to avoid drawing attention to their whereabouts. The young are weaned at 16–22 days and sexually mature at 2–3 months, by which time they have already dispersed. They may live up to 10 years in captivity but rarely longer then 3 years in the wild.

LIFESTYLE: Cottontails are bad-tempered and intolerant of one another. Their individual home ranges overlap slightly, but females defend a core area around their breeding nest and will repel intruders aggressively. Male ranges overlap those of several females but the male must conduct a protracted courtship before any female will tolerate his presence long enough to mate. Both males and females use scent from glands in the cheeks to mark their area.

An ideal territory includes a mosaic of habitats with plenty of food and cover. However cottontails are extremely adaptable and do well in many habitats in spite of centuries of persecution in some areas.

Cottontails are naturally resistant to the viral disease myxomatosis (unlike European rabbits), but large numbers are preyed upon by carnivores and birds of prey.

Cottontails are mainly nocturnal but they are sometimes active by day, especially in summer when the nights are short. In winter they remain active and do not hibernate.

ON THE ALERT
Cottontails are alert and nervous animals, with sharp eyes and acute hearing. They can remain perfectly still, their dull brown fur serving as camouflage.

WESTERN EUROPEAN HEDGEHOG

Erinaceus europaeus
Family: ERINACEIDAE
Order: INSECTIVORA

DISTRIBUTION: Open woodlands, hedges, grasslands, parks and other urban areas of western Europe and Russia.

SIZE: Length 10–12in (25–30cm); tail 0.8–1.2in (2–3cm); weight 0.9–2.2lb (0.4–1.1kg).

APPEARANCE: A short legged animal with a pointed snout and small beady eyes. The body is covered in sharp brown spines tipped with yellow, which grow through the normal hair. The face, legs and belly are not spiny.

DIET: Mostly invertebrates found on or just below the ground, plus some larger prey including frogs, snakes, baby birds and small mammals. They also eat carrion and food scraps left out by people.

BREEDING: Hedgehogs are capable of breeding twice a year, usually between May and October. Litters of 2–10 babies arrive after a gestation lasting 31–37 days and

are cared for by their mother in a nest of leaves and grass. The babies are weaned at 38–45 days and reach sexual maturity at about 10 months. Longevity is anything up to 7 years.

LIFESTYLE: Hedgehogs are generally solitary. Adult males occupy home ranges of around 75 acres (30 ha), which overlap smaller ranges of about 25 acres (10ha) occupied by females. The animals are very active at night, often traveling more than a mile back and forth around their range. They avoid meeting up with their neighbors but use scent to communicate their whereabouts. They also go to considerable trouble covering their own body with saliva – producing foamy spit and flicking it over its spines with its tongue. This strange behavior, known as "self anointing" is not properly understood – it happens mostly in the breeding season but also when the animal is anxious. Hedgehogs put on weight in summer and early fall and rely on stored fat to see them through the winter, when they hibernate in a specially build nest of leaves. Young hedgehogs born late in the summer face a race against time. It is imperative they put on as much weight as possible before winter arrives and forces them into hibernation. Underweight hedgehogs remain active much later in the fall than well-fed adults.

BALL POINT
Hedgehogs rely on their dense coat of spines to protect them from most predators. From a young age they know how to curl into a tight ball, tucking their face and legs out of harm's way should a predator approach. They wait until they sense that danger has passed. It is a highly effective defense mechanism.

COMMON SHREW

Sorex araneus
Family: SORICIDAE
Order: INSECTIVORA

DISTRIBUTION: From Britain to western China. Shrews prefer damp places but occur in habitats as varied as forest, farmland, hedgerow, and tundra.

SIZE: Length: 2–3.2in (5–8cm); tail about 1in (2.5–3cm); weight 0.2–0.5oz (5–15g).

APPEARANCE: A tiny, brown mammal with a pointed twitchy nose, a thin tail, small ears and tiny black eyes. The fur of the belly is pale gray or beige.

DIET: Mostly insect larvae, worms and other soil invertebrates amounting to about 90 percent of the shrew's own bodyweight daily.

BREEDING: Breeding is frenetic, with up to 4 litters of 5, 6 or more young born in a single season between April and September. The combined weight of the babies often approaches that of the mother herself. She cares for them in a nest of loosely woven vegetation. The young are weaned at 3–4 weeks and earlier litters begin the same season. Maximum longevity is 14 months, and few shrews survive even a full year.

LIFESTYLE: Shrews do not live long, but their short lives are action-packed. They are constantly on the go, rushing from place to place, shoving their long, pointed nose into every nook and cranny and sniffing busily for food. Their sensitive whiskers detect movements of prey and they have highly sensitive hearing. They are active day and night, alternating bouts of frenzied activity with short naps every two hours or so. They need to eat almost constantly to fuel their rapid metabolism. Fortunately most shrew food is easy to find.

Shrews are solitary, highly territorial and very bad tempered. Each territory is about 500 square yards (420sq m), and the resident shrew is diligent in marking its

FAST BREEDERS
Female shrews give birth to
huge families. There can be
as many as 10 young in
a litter.

borders with scent and urine.
Encounters between neighbors are
almost always accompanied by high
pitched shrieking. The pitch and
intensity of the calls – some
inaudible to the human ear and
known as "ultrasound" – are thought
to convey dominance information
and sometimes help avoid fights. At
other times the protagonists rear up
on their hind legs and scratch at
each other, sometimes wrestling
and rolling over and over. Once the
bout is settled, the victor drives the
loser away and both go right back
to feeding. Hostilities are tem-
porarily lifted during the breeding
season, but courtship and mating
are brief and often very rough.

Common shrews have glands in
the skin which secrete substances
distasteful to potential predators.

STAR-NOSED MOLE

Condylura cristata
Family: TALPIDAE
Order: INSECTIVORA

DISTRIBUTION: The star-nosed mole is found in damp meadows, woods and marshes near lakes, and rivers and streams in the northeastern United States south to Georgia, and southeastern Canada from Labrador to Manitoba.

SIZE: Length: 4–5in (10–12cm); tail 2.2–3.3in (5.6–8.4cm); weight 1.4–3oz (40–84g).

APPEARANCE: A small black animal with a cylindrical body, a thin, hairy tail and short legs. The front legs are powerful with large hands. The most remarkable feature of this creature is a cluster of about 22 pink, fleshy, hairless and finger-like projections at the tip of the snout around the nostrils. These become fatter in both sexes in winter; they

are thought to contain fat reserves for the breeding season. The fur is dense and water-repellent.

DIET: Invertebrates, mainly earthworms found in the soil, also small freshwater fish and insect larvae caught while swimming.

BREEDING: Females breed once a year, producing up to 7 young in early summer. The exact gestation period is unknown. The young are reared in a large nest of dry vegetation, usually built above ground level. They begin to disperse at just 3–4 weeks old and become sexually mature after about 11 months. Longevity is probably about 5 years.

LIFESTYLE: Star-nosed moles live underground in tunnels that they dig with their large square hands, shoving excavated soil to the surface, forming molehills. The tunnels are often very shallow – in wet ground deep burrows would be prone to flooding. The tunnel systems usually have several entrances, at least one of which may be underwater. The moles usually live alone in their tunnels and patrol regularly to collect invertebrates that drop in from the surrounding soil. The moles are active by day and night all year around and often forage above ground and in the water. In winter they will dive under the ice and forage in tunnels beneath the snow.

FLESHY PROJECTIONS
The fleshy projections on the mole's nose are sensitive to touch and possibly also to minute electrical disturbances emanating from the moving bodies of small prey animals. The projections can also be used to hold and manipulate the mole's food.

THREE-TOED SLOTH

Bradypus varigatus
Family: BRADYPODIDAE
Order: XENARTHRA

DISTRIBUTION: In forests of Central and South America from Honduras to northern parts of Argentina.

SIZE: Length 16–27in (42–70cm); tail 1–3.5in (2–9cm); weight 5–12lb (2–6kg).

APPEARANCE: A long-legged, shaggy-coated animal with a very short tail and a small, round head. The hands and feet are hooklike with long, curved claws. The fur is brown but often has a greenish hue due to the growth of algae in grooves in the shaft of each hair.

DIET: Leaves, buds, and other parts of *Cecropia* trees.

BREEDING: Females give birth to single young at any time of year after a 5–6 month gestation period. The baby clings to its mother's front and is suckled for 3–4 weeks. After that it begins feeding itself but it cannot climb on its own until it is 5 months old.

LIFESTYLE: The three-toed sloth is famous for its slow movement. It spends virtually its whole life wedged in the fork of a tree or suspended from branches with its hooklike hands and gets about by shuffling along hand over hand. The long legs are too weak to support the animal's bodyweight properly standing up, and sloths on the ground are extremely vulnerable. Nevertheless they do descend to the forest floor every few days in order to shuffle to another tree. Strangely they also urinate and defecate on the ground. Sloths live alone and while they are not actively territorial, they seem to avoid each other's company.

An unusual feature is that a sloth has 2 or 3 extra vertebrae in the neck, allowing it to rotate its head three-quarters of the way around, like an owl. This means it can see all around and reach for awkwardly placed leaves without having to move its body.

HIDDEN AWAY
Sloths rely on their camouflage coats and slow movements to hide them from view, and remain high in the trees where they are less likely to be spotted.

NINE-BANDED ARMADILLO

Dasypus novemcinctatus
Family: DASYPODIDAE
Order: XENARTHRA

DISTRIBUTION: Originally from Central and South America south to Uruguay and west to Peru, the species has successfully colonized the southern USA in the last 200 years. It is also found on Grenada, Trinidad and Tobago in the West Indies. It occupies grassland, forests, and farmland.

SIZE: Length 14–22in (35.5–57cm); tail 1–1.75in (2.5–4.5cm); weight: 6–17lb (2.7–7.7kg). Males usually grow bigger than females.

APPEARANCE: A small, stout animal with bony armor plating. The back, head, legs and long tail are scaly. The head is small with long naked ears and a pointed snout. There are 8–11 flexible bands around the middle of the body – the species is named for the northern Central American variety, which almost always has 9 bands.

DIET: Mostly insects, especially termites, beetles and their larvae, but also worms, snails, bird eggs, small vertebrates, fruits, fungi, and carrion.

BREEDING: Reproduction is unusual in that all young born in a litter (usually 4 of them) are genetically identical, having developed from a single fertilized egg. Females give

BOLDLY GOING
Armadillos are bold. They forage by day, out in the open in safety because their natural armor will protect them. But their habit of curling up when disturbed makes them easy for humans to catch.

birth in spring after 120 days gestation, and suckle their babies for 4–5 months. Most begin breeding after 1 year. Captives have lived at least 22 years but longevity in the wild is probably less.

LIFESTYLE: The armadillo is mainly active in the late evening and at night. It shuffles about slowly, nose to the ground, snorting frequently as it sniffs for prey. If threatened it curls up in a tight ball so that its vulnerable underside is protected by bony plates. When foraging, it moves slowly, snuffling and grunting almost continuously as it rummages for food in grass and leaf litter. It has an excellent sense of smell and is an accomplished digger. Its strong-clawed feet can also break open rotting logs.

Armadillos live alone, but are tolerant of each other. The home ranges of different animals often overlap. They may dig their own burrow or they may move into existing ones.

RODRIGUES FLYING FOX

Pteropus rodricensis
Family: PTEROPODIDAE
Order: CHIROPTERA

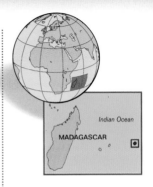

Indian Ocean

MADAGASCAR

DISTRIBUTION: Occurs only on Rodrigues Island, near Mauritius in the Indian Ocean. The bats roost in dry palm woodlands. The entire population numbers less than 2,000 making it "Critically Endangered."

SIZE: Length 6in (15cm); wingspan 36in (90cm); weight 12–13oz (350g).

APPEARANCE: A large fruit bat with a pointed foxy face, dark brown fur except on the shoulders, which are usually dark gold. The wings are black and fold neatly at the bat's sides when resting.

DIET: Ripe fruit, flowers, leaves and pollen, but little solid food is ingested. The bat pulps the food in its mouth, swallows the juice and spits out the solids.

BREEDING: The females can only rear just one baby a year. Young bats are born between August and September and spend the first few weeks of life clinging to their mother, being carried wherever she goes. As they get heavier they are increasingly left in the roost while the mothers go out to feed.

LIFESTYLE: Among the world's most threatened bats. Being naturally restricted to one small island and dependent on mixed forest for food and roosts, they are vulnerable to natural disasters and have suffered from the spread of plantations. They live in colonies and the colonial daytime roosts are noisy places. The resident bats are constantly fidgeting, jostling and calling out to one another. At dusk they fly off to feeding areas and may spend several hours hanging in a feeding tree digesting the fruit they have eaten before flying back to the roost around dawn.

FRUIT DISPERSER
Flying foxes play a
vital role in forest
ecology, dispersing
seeds from the fruit
they eat and
pollinating flowers
they visit at night.
They drink on the
wing and sometimes
swoop down to sip
sea water –
presumably to
supplement their
salt intake.

SMOKY BAT

Furipterus horrens
Family: FURIPTERIDAE
Order: CHIROPTERA

DISTRIBUTION: Old growth rain forest in Central and northern South America from Costa Rica to Brazil.

SIZE: Length 1.3–1.5in (3.3–4cm); wingspan about 8in (21cm); tail 1–1.5in (2.4–3.6cm); weight 0.1oz (3g).

APPEARANCE: A tiny bat with broad wings and a deep tail membrane. The fur is very soft and a variable shade of gray. The eyes are tiny and hidden in the fur; the ears are large, funnel-shaped and furry. The bat has a much reduced thumb, which is enclosed within a wing membrane so that only the small claw protrudes. Wings and legs are relatively long. The snout is piglike and slightly upturned.

DIET: Moths and other night-flying insects.

BREEDING: Reproduction is little known in this species. Females produce one baby at a time, which spends the first few weeks of life clinging to her fur. The female's teats are low down on her abdomen, not on the chest or armpit as in most other bats. While the mother roosts upside down, the baby rests the other way up with its head tucked into her groin.

LIFESTYLE: This little-known species is one of two closely related South American smoky bats. They roost communally in hollow trees and caves and often share such spaces with other species of bat. The composition of roosting colonies seems to vary with season. All-male roosts have been found in May, while mixed sex groups of adults and young are recorded in January. Sometimes the members of a colony are tightly clustered, at other times more widely spaced. This may be to do with temperature regulation or it may be that mothers with young are protective and prefer to avoid close contact.

They hunt close to water. They are easily disturbed. Resting colonies take flight at the first sign of disturbance. They fly quite low, and the flight pattern is slow and not unlike that of the moths they hunt. Prey is detected using echolocation and caught on the wing. The bat's large tail membrane may be used to scoop large insects out of the air and carry them to a perch where they can be eaten.

SIGHT UNSEEN
Smoky bats' eyes are very small and almost completely obscured by the ears and facial fur. Their sight is poor, but they can navigate and hunt effectively using echolocation to detect objects around them.

225

GREATER HORSESHOE BAT

> *Rhinolophus ferrumequinum*
> Family: RHINOLOPHIDAE
> Order: CHIROPTERA

DISTRIBUTION: In woodlands, caves, and scrub close to open grassland and water throughout the temperate and subtropical Old World northern hemisphere including southern Britain, central and southern Europe, North Africa, the Middle East, and Asia to Japan.

SIZE: Length 2.2–2.8in (5.7–7.1cm); wingspan 11–13.5in (2–35cm); tail 1.4–1.7in (3.5–4.3cm); weight 0.5–1.2oz (14–34g). Males are half as big again as females.

APPEARANCE: A small-bodied bat with long, narrow wings. The fur is very soft and fluffy, usually grayish brown with a reddish tinge on the back. The face is dominated by large ears and a fleshy horseshoe-shaped structure called the "nose leaf", used for focusing the sounds produced for echolocation.

DIET: Large, nocturnal, flying insects such as moths and beetles.

BREEDING: Mating occurs prior to hibernation in the fall and females store sperm until they ovulate in spring. Gestation lasts about 7 weeks and young are born in summer. They develop quickly and are able to fly and catch insects within one month. They are weaned at about 6 weeks and fully independent at 8 weeks. Females cannot rear more than 1 young a year and most do not begin breeding until they are at least 3 or 4 years old. Horseshoe bats may survive up to 30 years.

LIFESTYLE: Greater horseshoe bats live in communal roosts and sleep by day, hanging upside down with their wings folded about them. In summer these roosts will be in caves or in buildings such as barns, churches, or houses with lofts, within about 6 miles (10km) of good feeding areas.

In winter, hibernation roosts are usually in very deep caves or mine

shafts where the air is still and the temperature remains more or less constant all winter. Hibernating bats often cluster together, presumably to reduce heat loss and thereby save energy. Periods of warm weather will wake them up and they emerge to feed on whatever insects might be around.

LISTENING FOR PREY
Horseshoe bats emerge to hunt about an hour after sunset. They detect prey by echolocation (producing pulses of sound in the nostrils and listening for the echoes bouncing off other objects).

LONG-NOSED ECHIDNA

Zaglossus bruijni
Family: TACHYGLOSSIDAE
Order: MONOTREMATA

DISTRIBUTION: Found only on the island of New Guinea, in humid woodland and meadows.

SIZE: Length 17.5–30in (45–77.5cm); weight 11–22lb (5–10kg) – considerably larger than the better-known short-beaked echidna of Australia.

APPEARANCE: A squat, rotund animal with short legs and only the barest suggestion of a tail. The face is drawn out into a long, tapering, slightly down-curved snout covered with rubbery skin. The body is covered in light brown to brownish-black hairs, which may be dense or very sparse. Among the hairs, everywhere but the snout and belly, are hundreds of blunt spines, ranging in color from white to black. Females have no teats.

DIET: Earthworms and other soil invertebrates.

BREEDING: Female echidnas probably produce 4–6 young in a litter. The babies are born inside eggs but hatch soon afterward and are thenceforth carried in a small temporary pouch where they feed on milk seeping from mammary ducts. Weaning period is not known, but sexual maturity comes at about 1 year. Longevity may be in excess of 30 years.

LIFESTYLE: The long-nosed echidna is principally nocturnal and emerges at dusk to spend the night shuffling around the forest floor and rummaging in the leaf litter for food. While short-beaked echidnas eat ants and termites and lap them up using a long tongue, this species favors earthworms. The tongue only emerges about 1 inch (2.5cm) beyond the end of the echidna's snout but it has rows of toothlike spines arranged in a groove running down the middle. These spines are used to snare the worm and the powerful tongue muscles then haul the worm from its burrow.

As far as is known, long-nosed echidnas live alone in well-spaced home ranges. They rest in hollow logs, rock crevices, and burrows and their large feet and strong claws are superbly adapted for digging. They cannot move very fast but are relatively safe from predators because of their covering of tough spines. These can be erected at will, and help to wedge the animal when it is burrowing.

ACUTE SENSES
Echidnas have small eyes and their sight is not terribly good. Their hearing however is acute and their sense of smell is excellent. The snout's rubbery skin is highly sensitive.

PLATYPUS

Ornithorhynchus anatinus
Family: ORNITHORHYNCHIDAE
Order: MONOTREMATA

DISTRIBUTION: Freshwater streams and pools in Eastern Australia, including parts of Tasmania, New South Wales, Victoria, South Australia and Queensland. Thanks to conservation efforts, platypus numbers are increasing and the species is re-establishing itself in many waterways, even in cities.

SIZE: Length 12–18in (30–45cm); tail 4–6in (10–15cm); weight 1.1–4.4lb (0.5–2kg). Average size varies considerably with range, but males almost always larger than females.

APPEARANCE: A bizarre-looking animal, with a torpedo-shaped body, paddle-like tail, short legs and large webbed feet and a soft, rubbery beak. Males are armed with sharp spurs on their hind leg ankles. The dark brown coat is dense and woolly.

DIET: Small aquatic animals, especially crustaceans, insect larvae, worms, fish, and tadpoles, which the platypus detects using electricity sensors in its bill.

BREEDING: Females lay 1 to 3 sticky eggs the size of large marbles in a damp chamber at the end of a long burrow. Tiny, underdeveloped young hatch after 10 days and are brooded for a further 4 months in the nest burrow. They lap milk seeping from glands in the mother's belly – there are no teats. The young are weaned at 4 months, sexually mature at 2 or 3 years, and may live up to 14 years in the wild.

LIFESTYLE: Despite its placid appearance, this is the world's only venomous mammal. Males fight in the water using sharp spurs on their rear ankles that can deliver a toxin powerful enough to kill a dog.
  Platypus usually spend the day in inconspicuous burrows in the banks of pools and streams and emerge

to feed at dusk. Most of their waking hours are spent in water, a medium to which they are superbly well adapted. The platypus has reasonable eyesight and hearing, but underwater the eyes and ears are closed and the platypus relies solely on its bill for sensory input. The bill is moist and rubbery, and covered in minute pits lined with sensitive nerve endings that detect the tiny electrical fields generated by the bodies of small animals.

The platypus is for the most part a solitary animal. Individuals living nearby avoid meeting up, except during the spring, when males compete aggressively for females.

SECRETIVE SWIMMER
Platypus swim silently at the surface, using their front feet for propulsion, the hind ones for steering and braking. Under water they move much faster and with great agility. Dives rarely last more than a minute.

VIRGINIA OPOSSUM

Didelphis virginiana
Family: DIDELPHIDAE
Order: DIDELPHIMORPHIA

DISTRIBUTION: North America's only native marsupial mammal, the Virginia opossum is common in wooded areas or scrub close to water throughout the eastern and central United States. It was introduced on the west coast in 1890 and has spread from California to southern Canada. It is also found to the south through much of Central America to Nicaragua. There are 63 species of American opossums distributed in North, South, and Central America, ranging from cat- to mouse-size.

SIZE: Length 13–20in (35–55cm); tail 10–21.5in (25–54cm); weight 4.5–12lb (2–5.5 kg).

APPEARANCE: This charismatic cat-sized animal has a shaggy looking coat of white-tipped hairs, short legs and a long, prehensile, mostly hairless tail. Its face is pointed, with a pink nose, long whiskers, big black eyes and prominent oval ears. Its paws are strong and dexterous with a first toe that comes together in a grasping action. Females have a well-developed pouch containing 13 teats.

DIET: Plant and animal matter, living and dead. Opossums often scavenge from human refuse.

BREEDING: Females produce huge litters, usually about 20 young, but sometimes as many as 56, after a gestation of just 13 days. There are only enough teats in the pouch for 13 young – the rest will die. Juveniles emerge from the pouch at 70 days and are fully weaned at 3–4 months. Opossums reach sexual maturity at 6–8 months. Mortality is high and few survive more than 3 years in the wild.

LIFESTYLE: Virginia opossums live alone in large home ranges. They do not defend a territory, but are highly antisocial and aggressive to other opossums they meet. Even courtship is brief and perfunctory and pairs separate as soon as mating is over.

Opossums sleep by day in grass nests wedged in tree holes and crevices. Often they are partly nomadic, moving around as seasonal feeding opportunities come and go. In summer they often grow extremely fat. They do not hibernate and fat reserves can prove crucial to winter survival. Opossums use the remarkable tactic of playing dead when threatened, remaining utterly unresponsive (catatonic) for anything up to six hours.

CLIMBING TO SUCCESS
Opossums are excellent climbers, helped greatly by their long grasping tail – this is so strong the animal can hang from the tail alone. The opossum's feet are highly dexterous, and can be used to grip and manipulate objects while feeding.

NUMBAT

Myrmecobius fasciatus
Family: MYRMECOBIIDAE
Order: DASYUROMORPHIA

AUSTRALIA

DISTRIBUTION: Protected areas of southwestern Western Australia, in open eucalypt woodland and scrub. Numbats have been saved from extinction by intensive conservation measures, but the total population is still just a few thousand.

SIZE: Length 6.5–10.5in (17–2cm); tail 5–8in (13–21cm); weight: 0.7–1.4lb (300–650g).

APPEARANCE: Vaguely squirrel-like animal with long, tapering, furry tail and large feet with long claws. It is unusually boldly patterned for a marsupial. It has gray fur on the belly, red-brown on the back, and is marked with 6 or 7 white bars on the rump (between the mid-back and the base of the tail), and has whitish underparts. These patterns give it a striped appearance and help break up its outline in strong dappled sunlight. The muzzle is long and pointed with a small black nose, ears are erect; eyes are large and black, and a dark stripe runs across the sides of the face like a bandit mask. The numbat has more teeth than any other land-dwelling mammal – up to 52.

DIET: Almost exclusively termites. Mounds or nests in trees and dead wood are opened using strong claws and the insects lapped up with a highly mobile tongue about 4 inches (10cm) long.

BREEDING: Tiny young are born in summer in litters of 2–4 after just 14 days gestation. Females have 4 teats hidden among long belly fur, but no pouch. Newborns spend 4 months attached to a teat with well-developed mouth muscles, then a further 2 months in a secure nest. They are weaned at 6 months, sexually mature and independent from 9 months.

LIFESTYLE: The numbat is very active and nimble. It climbs well and, unusually for a marsupial, is active in daytime, because the termites it feeds on are also active only during the day. Adults are solitary, occupying relatively large home ranges of up to 370 acres (150ha). Communication is mainly by scent, but individuals will utter hissing sounds when disturbed.

Numbats use burrows or hollow logs for sleeping and nesting. They may live for up to 6 years.

WOOD LOVER
Numbats live in open sunny woodlands with plenty of dead wood. Fallen logs are usually infested with the termites on which these marsupials feed.

TASMANIAN DEVIL

Sarcophilus harrisii
Family: DASYURIDAE
Order: DASYUROMORPHIA

AUSTRALIA

Tasmania

DISTRIBUTION: Tasmanian Devils were once widespread in Australia, but suffered greatly from persecution and competition from introduced carnivores. They are now restricted to heaths and forests on the island state of Tasmania.

SIZE: Length 21–31.5in (53–80cm); height up to 12in (30cm); tail 9–12in (23–30cm); weight 9–26lb (4–12kg). Males grow bigger than females.

APPEARANCE: A squat, barrel-bodied animal like a little bear, with a heavy-looking, muscular head, powerful jaws, a short furry tail and relatively slender legs. The coat is grayish-brown, sometimes with a darker stripe along midline of back; underparts whitish. Males sometimes all-white. Both sexes have a yellow rim around the eyes. The ears are hairless and prominent and the tail is naked and prehensile. Females have a small, rear-opening pouch.

DIET: Tasmanian devils are out-and-out carnivores – the name Sarcophilus means flesh-lover. They eat mostly carrion in the form of dead wallabies, wombats, sheep, and rabbits; they can even chew and swallow sheep bones. They hunt smaller vertebrate and invertebrate prey for themselves.

BREEDING: Devils begin breeding at 2 years of age, and females produce litters of 2–4 young in the fall after a short pregnancy of 31 days. The young spend 3 months in the pouch and continue being suckled for a further 5 months. They live about 6 years.

LIFESTYLE: A Tasmanian devil in a feeding frenzy is all gaping jaws, sharp teeth and wild eyes. Devils were so named by early European settlers who witnessed them fighting furiously over the carcasses of other animals, blood-spattered and snarling and ripping out great chunks of meat which they swallowed without chewing. For the most part however, these

are surprisingly peaceful animals. They are not the wanton killers they were once perceived to be – they eat mostly carrion and rarely kill anything larger than a rabbit. Only when several devils converge on prey do things get ugly.

Most of the time devils live alone, each one occupying a home range of between 3 to 8 square miles (8–20sq km). They sleep by day in hollow logs or the abandoned burrows of other animals, and hunt by night, ambling along and investigating every likely spot with noisy snuffling.

MEAT-EATING MARSUPIAL
The Tasmanian devil is the largest surviving carnivorous marsupial. It is now a protected species and the symbol of the Tasmanian Wildlife Service.

COMMON RINGTAIL POSSUM

Pseudocheirus peregrinus
Family: PSEUDOCHEIRIDAE
Order: DIPROTODONTIA

DISTRIBUTION: Eastern Australia from far northern Queensland to southeastern South Australia and Tasmania.

SIZE: Length 12–13.5in (30–35cm); tail 12–13.5in (30–35cm); weight 1.5–2.4lb (0.7–1.1kg).

APPEARANCE: A cat-sized animal with dense, soft fur and a long, tapering prehensile tail often held coiled into a ring. The tip of the tail is white, except for a bare patch on the underside, which provides grip. There are white patches behind the ears and the rest of the body is a variable shade of brown or gray. The eyes are large, the ears furry and rounded.

DIET: Leaves, fruit, sap, buds, and other plant material, and insects.

BREEDING: Females rear 1 or 2 litters of 1–3 young a year, but the season varies in different parts of the species range. The young spend 14–18 weeks in the pouch and become fully independent at 8–12 months. Longevity in the wild is usually 4–5 years, though captives have lived a lot longer.

LIFESTYLE: Common ringtail possums are strictly nocturnal. They spend the day resting in spherical nests woven from twigs and leaves and wedged in thickets or high up in the branches of trees. These nests are often built in clusters and the owners interact peacefully as long as food is plentiful. Overcrowding leads to increased aggression. The home ranges of males are larger than those of females and though pair bonds often last more than one season, males will seek additional pairings after their first mate has given birth.

In some parts of the species' range, eucalyptus leaves form a large part of the diet. These are difficult to digest and very low in nutritional value. The possum's gut

SAFETY FIRST
Ringtails are excellent climbers and spend almost all their time in trees. They move slowly and carefully, using their prehensile tail as a safety rope and only releasing it from a hold once they have gained a firm grip on a new perch with their feet.

is long, but the leaves are only partially digested by the time they are excreted. In order to get the most out of these meager rations the possum eats its first droppings, which are soft and green. After a second passage through the gut the droppings are dry and hard and every possible morsel of goodness has been absorbed.

If disturbed, ringtail possums tend to freeze and gaze straight ahead with an unblinking stare. They may stay like that for several minutes before moving slowly away.

KOALA

Phascolarctos cinereus
Family: PHASCOLARCTIDAE
Order: DIPROTODONTIA

DISTRIBUTION: Koalas have a patchy distribution in eucalypt forest and scrub in Eastern Australia. They are protected by law but many populations are overcrowded and subject to controversial culls.

SIZE: Length 23.5–33.5in (60–86cm); weight 9–33lb (4–15kg). Males are larger than females and southern specimens larger than their northern cousins. There is no visible tail.

APPEARANCE: The closest thing to a live teddy bear, the koala has thick, woolly, grayish-brown fur, a large head with round fluffy ears, beady eyes and large black nose. The tail is a short stump but the legs are long and very strong, with five large claws on each foot. The female has a backward-opening pouch.

DIET: Leaves and bark of various Eucalyptus species, digested with the aid of gut-dwelling bacteria.

Young koalas ("joeys") are weaned on leaves already partially digested by the mother.

BREEDING: Tiny joeys are born after 25–30 days gestation and spend 5–7 months in the pouch. After that they ride on their mothers back until they are fully weaned at 6–12 months. Longevity can be as long as 18 years in the wild.

LIFESTYLE: Koalas are the only mammals than can make a living eating eucalyptus, a plant with very little nutrient value. They manage by having an incredibly low energy lifestyle. They sleep wedged in a forked branch for up to 20 hours a day and spend most of the other four hours eating.

Koalas live in overlapping home ranges but ignore their neighbors for most of the year. They may use the same favorite trees but at different times. During the

breeding season however, large males become aggressively territorial, evicting smaller individuals and claiming the resident females as their own. Today's scattered populations are now at risk from forest fires and many koalas are also killed on roads as they climb down from their trees to seek out new homes.

TREE SAFETY
Koalas spend very little time on the ground, generally only coming down to swap trees or to seek out a new home.

COMMON WOMBAT

Vombatus ursinus
Family: VOMBATIDAE
Order: DIPROTODONTIA

DISTRIBUTION: Open forests and scrub in southeastern Australia.

SIZE: Length 27.5–47in (70–120cm); weight 33–77lb (15–35kg).

APPEARANCE: A squat, solidly built animal. The wombat has a very short tail, long, strong claws, a large, heavy-looking head and a coat of coarse brown fur. The female has a pouch, which opens to the rear so that it does not fill with soil when burrowing.

DIET: Plant material including leaves, stems, and roots, also fungi, grasses, and herbs. As in rodents, the teeth grow continuously to make up for the wear caused by tough plant fibers.

BREEDING: Females give birth to just one young (very occasionally twins) every 2 years. Gestation is 21 days and the baby spends a further 2–3 months developing in the pouch before it faces the outside world. The mother continues to suckle her youngster until it is 15 months old. Wombats can live well into their 20s.

LIFESTYLE: Wombats have short, powerful legs adapted for digging and they build impressive burrows up to 100 feet (30m) long, with several different chambers and entrances. There are often several such dens within a wombat's home range – an area of between 12 to 57 acres (3–23ha). Common wombats live alone and are intolerant of intruders. They leave scent on landmarks such as logs and boulders within their home range. Males become more aggressive during the breeding season. They fight by kicking with their hind legs and use the same technique for warding off their predators, such as dogs.

The wombat's diet of plant tissues is rather poor, with low energy value. It makes the most of every mouthful by digesting it slowly. Wombats live low-energy lives, resting often and making use of the sun's heat to warm themselves by basking on chilly winter mornings. The diet contains little water, and in hot weather the wombat must conserve moisture as well as energy. In summer they are almost entirely nocturnal. They stay below ground during the heat of the day, so they don't lose precious water by sweating or evaporation.

ORIGINAL DIGGERS
Wombats are the world's largest burrowing mammals and have few enemies other than humans. They are sometimes persecuted as pests because of their industrious burrowing.

HONEY POSSUM

Tarsipes rostratus
Family: TARSIPEDIDAE
Order: DIPROTODONTIA

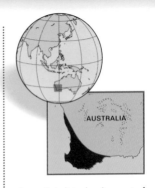

AUSTRALIA

DISTRIBUTION: Trees and shrubs in south-western Australia.

SIZE: Length 1.6–3.7in (4–9.5cm); tail 1.8–4.3in (4.5–11cm); weight 0.25–0.55oz (7–16g).

APPEARANCE: A tiny, mouselike marsupial with gray-brown fur and 3 dark dorsal stripes. The face is long and pointed. The tail is very long, with a hooked, prehensile tip and the feet have long fingers and toes with expanded tips – both are adaptations for climbing. The tongue is a quarter the length of the body. It ends in a brushlike tip.

DIET: The honey possum is one of the world's most specialized feeders. It can extend its tongue 1 inch (2.5cm) beyond its nose so that the bristles on its tip brush pollen and nectar from flowering trees and shrubs.

BREEDING: The young are born in litters of 2 or 3 after a gestation period of 21–28 days – plus up to

a 2-month halt in development of the embryo (called "embryonic diapause" that some bats, kangaroos, and possums are able to achieve). These are the smallest babies of any mammal, weighing less than 0.0002 ounces (5mg) each. They increase their birth weight 500 times in the first 8 weeks in the pouch and are weaned at 10 weeks. They are sexually mature at 10 months, but time to breed is short since few live longer than one year.

LIFESTYLE: Agile climbers, honey possums use their tiny, monkeylike hands and feet and prehensile tail to grip.

Among honey possums, females are socially dominant to males. They compete with one another for rank and territory. Dominant breeding females exclude others from their range, while subordinate females and males live in groups. Cohabitation is especially common in cold weather, when several animals will huddle together in a tree hole or other den. In winter, when pollen and nectar are scarce, honey possums may enter a deep sleep known as torpor and so not use up valuable energy levels.

GRIPPING TAIL
Honey possums live in trees and are active mainly at night. The tail is strong enough to support the animal's whole weight dangling from a twig.

QUOKKA

Setonix brachyurus
Family: MACROPODIDAE
Order: DIPROTODONTIA

DISTRIBUTION: Extreme south western Australia, especially on Rottnest and Bald Islands, where there are no introduced predators.

SIZE: Length 15.5–21in (40–54cm); tail 9.5–12in (24.5–31cm); weight 6–9.3lb (2.7–4.2kg).

APPEARANCE: A small chubby-looking wallaby with a short, ratlike tail. The face is short and pointed, with short furry ears and large eyes. The slightly grizzled brown fur is thick and coarse.

DIET: Mostly plant material, but island quokkas have also learned to scavenge from tourists.

BREEDING: Quokkas are capable of breeding at any time of year in good conditions but those living on islands do not attempt to do so during the long dry summers. Single young are born after 26–28 days gestation and spend about 6 months in the pouch, and a further 3–4 months returning periodically to suckle. They usually breed in their second year. Female quokkas mate a second time immediately after giving birth and maintain the resulting embryo in a state of suspended animation. It will only develop and be born if the baby in the pouch should die very young.

LIFESTYLE: Hunted almost to extinction by introduced predators, quokkas now live only on protected reserves and offshore islands. The island quokkas have had to adapt to different lifestyles to those on the mainland. The main problem for island quokkas is drought. There are no rivers or streams on Rottnest Island, only several very salty lagoons. In order to survive the hot summer the quokkas converge on areas with rainwater soaks and dense vegetation providing shade. There is intense competition for these precious resources and the animals living around a water soak deny access to nonlocals. At other times of year the quokkas are more tolerant and spread out over a wide range of habitat types.

AT THE HOP
Like all members of the kangaroo and wallaby family, quokkas have strongly developed hind-quarters for hopping, aided by a muscular tail for balance and maneuvering.

EASTERN GRAY KANGAROO

Macropus giganteus
Family: MACROPODIDAE
Order: DIPROTODONTIA

DISTRIBUTION: Scrub, woodland and forest in areas in wetter parts of eastern Australia including parts of Queensland, New South Wales and Victoria, South Australia and Tasmania.

SIZE: Length 33–55in (0.85–1.4m); height up to 6ft (1.8m); tail 30–39in (0.75–1m); weight 44–145lb (20–66kg). Males taller and much heavier than females.

APPEARANCE: This large kangaroo has coarse silvery-gray fur, darker on the face, tail, legs and feet and paler in the belly. The female has a large forward-opening pouch.

DIET: Grass and other plant material.

BREEDING: Baby kangaroos (called "joeys") are born one a time and incubated in the pouch for 11 months, during which time the mother is usually carrying her next baby in a state of suspended development called "embryonic diapause" that some bats kangaroos, and possums are able to achieve). Joeys are weaned at 18 months and the females may begin breeding soon after. Young males, however, may not gain sufficient status to breed until they are 4 or 5 years old. Eastern grays live up to 20 years in the wild.

LIFESTYLE: Eastern gray kangaroos live in casual non-territorial groups known as mobs, made up of smaller, more closely knit family units comprising females and their subadult offspring. Adult males move from group to group, spending most time in mobs where one or more females are coming into heat. Large males dominate smaller ones and hence secure more matings, but they do not keep females in a harem.

Gray kangaroos are active at night, and retreat to shady woodland and scrub to rest during the day. They are less tolerant of heat and drought than red kangaroos, but cope well with cold – those living in Tasmania are especially hardy. When moving slowly this kangaroo uses its tail as a fifth limb. The tail helps the front legs by taking the animal's weight as the back legs swing forward.

FASTEST MARSUPIAL
The Eastern gray kangaroo is the fastest marsupial, outrunning the wallabies and other kangaroos. The powerful back legs, used for hopping, take this mammal at full speed to over 35mph (55kmh).

GLOSSARY

ADAPTATION features of an animal that adjust it to its environment; may be produced by evolution, e.g., camouflage coloration.

ADULT a fully grown sexually mature animal.

ALGAE primitive plants ranging from microscopic to seaweeds, but lacking proper roots or leaves.

ALPINE living in mountainous areas, over 5,000ft (1,500m).

AMPHIBIOUS able to live both on land and in water.

ANTLERS paired, branched structures made of bone and found only on the skull of the deer family. Antlers are shed annually.

AQUATIC living chiefly in water.

ARBOREAL living in trees.

BALEEN horny substance, commonly known as whalebone, growing as plates from the upper jaws of whales and forming a fringelike sieve to extract plankton from water.

BIODIVERSITY the variety of species and the variation within them.

BIOME a major world landscape characterized by having similar plants and animals living in it, e.g., desert, jungle, forest.

BIPED any animal that walks on two legs. Several species walk or hop short distances on two legs.

BREEDING SEASON the entire cycle of reproductive activity, from courtship, pair formation (and often establishment of territory) through nesting to independence of young.

CACHE a hidden store of food; also (verb) to hide food for future use.

CARNIVORE meat-eating animal.

CARRION rotting flesh of dead animals.

CLASS a large group of related animals. Mammals, insects, and reptiles are all classes of animals.

CLOUD FOREST moist, high-altitude forest characterized by a dense understory and an abundance of ferns, mosses, and other plants growing on the trunks and branches of trees. Home to many mammal species.

CONIFEROUS FOREST evergreen forests found in northern regions and mountainous areas, dominated by pines, spruce, and cedars.

CRUSTACEAN member of a class within the phylum Arthropoda typified by five pairs of legs, two pairs of antennae, a joined head and thorax, and calcerous deposits in the exoskeleton, e.g., crabs.

DECIDUOUS FOREST dominated by trees that lose their leaves in winter (or in the dry season).

DESERT area of low rainfall typically with sparse scrub or grassland vegetation or lacking it altogether.

DISPERSAL the scattering of young animals going to live away from where they were born and reared.

DIURNAL active during the day.

DOMESTICATION process of taming and breeding animals to provide help and useful products to humans.

ECOLOGY the study of plants and animals in relation to one another and to their surroundings.

ECOSYSTEM a whole system in which plants, animals, and their environment interact.

ENDEMIC found only in one geographical area, nowhere else.

ESTRUS relating to female mammals' reproductive cycle when they are receptive to mating with males. A looser term is "in heat."

EXTINCTION process of dying out at the end of which the very last individual dies, and the species is lost forever.

FAMILY a group of closely related genera that often also look quite similar. Zoological family names always end in -idae. Also used to describe a social group within a species comprising parents and their offspring.

FERAL living in the wild (refers to domestic animals such as dogs).

GENUS (genera, pl.) a group of closely related species.

GESTATION the period of pregnancy in mammals, between fertilization of the egg and birth of the baby.

HAREM a common social group in mammals made up of a single adult male with at least 2 female adults and several immature animals.

HERBIVORE an animal that eats plants by grazing and browsing.

HIBERNATION becoming inactive in winter, with lowered body temperature to save energy.

HOME RANGE the area in which an animal normally lives – whether or not the area is defended from other animals.

INCUBATION the act of keeping the egg or eggs warm or the period from the laying of eggs to hatching.

INDIGENOUS living naturally in a region; native (i.e. not an introduced species).

INSECTIVORE animal that feeds on insects, such as the anteater. Also used as a group name for hedgehogs, shrews, moles, and similar species.

INVERTEBRATES animals that have no backbone (or other bones) inside their body (insects, jellyfish).

JOEY a young kangaroo or a young koala.

JUVENILE a young animal that has not yet reached breeding age.

KRILL shrimp-like creatures found in large numbers in polar seas, forming main prey of baleen whales.

MAMMAL any animal of the class Mammalia – warm-blooded vertebrate having mammary glands in the female that produce milk with which it nurses its young. The class includes bats, primates, rodents, and whales.

MARINE living in the sea.

MARSUPIAL a unique group of mammals that suckle and protect newborns in an external pouch (the marsupium is the pouch).

MIGRATION movement from one place to another and back again; usually seasonal.

MONOTREME egg-laying mammal – echidnas and platypus, of the subclass Monotremata.

MONTANE a mountain environment.

NATURAL SELECTION the main process driving evolution in which animals and plants are challenged by natural effects (predators and bad weather), resulting in survival of the fittest.

NOCTURNAL active at night.

NOMADIC animals that wander continuously with no fixed home.

OMNIVORE animals that eat a wide range of animal and vegetable food.

ORDER a subdivision of a class of animals, consisting of a series of animal families.

ORGANISM any member of the animal or plant kingdom; a body that has life.

PARASITE an animal or plant that lives on or within the body of another (the host) from which it obtains nourishment. The host is often harmed by the association.

PHYLUM zoological term for a major grouping of animal classes. The whole animal kingdom is divided into about 30 phyla, of which the vertebrates form part of just one, the phylum Chordata.

PLANKTON minute animals and plants drifting in open water.

POPULATION a distinct group of animals of the same species or all the animals of that species.

PREDATOR an animal that kills live prey.

PREHENSILE being able to grasp, often refers to primates' tails.

PRIMARY FOREST forest that has always been forest and has not been cut down and regrown at some time.

PRIMATES a group of mammals that includes the monkeys and apes.

QUADRUPED any animal that walks on four legs.

RAIN FOREST tropical or subtropical forest with abundant and year-round rainfall.

RANGE the total geographical area over which a species is distributed.

RESIDENT an animal that inhabits, or resides in, a defined area, be it a home range or territory.

RODENT member of the order Rodentia, the largest mammalian order, which includes rats and mice, squirrels, porcupines, capybaras, and so on.

SAVANNA open grasslands with scattered trees and low rainfall, usually in warm areas.

SCRUB vegetation dominated by shrubs (woody plants usually with more than one stem).

SPECIES a group of mammals that are part of a genus with many similar features and structures and can breed and produce healthy young. Species are sometimes split into subspecies.

STEPPE open grassland in parts of the world where the climate is too harsh for trees to grow.

SUBSPECIES a subpopulation of a single species whose members are similar to each other but differ from the typical form for that species; often called a race.

TAIGA the northernmost coniferous forest with open, boggy, rocky areas in between.

TAXONOMY the branch of biology concerned with classifying organisms into groups according to similarities in their structure, origins, or behavior. The main categories, in order of increasing broadness, are: species, genus, family, order, class, phylum.

TERRESTRIAL living on land.

TERRITORY defended space.

TINE a point or projection on an antler.

TORPOR a short-term hibernation brought on by extreme cold or food shortage.

UNGULATE hoofed mammal; usually large and herbivorous.

VERTEBRATE animal with a backbone (e.g., fish, mammal, reptile), usually with skeleton made of bones, but sometimes softer cartilage.

VIVIPAROUS (of most mammals and a few other vertebrates) giving birth to active young – not laying eggs.

WARREN a communal series of burrows used by rabbits and squirrels.

ZOOLOGIST person who studies animals. (Zoology is the study of animals).

INDEX